TOP-RATED VIN

AND HOW TO USE THEM IN Y[...] GARDEN

This book was produced for Western Publishing Company, Inc., by the staff of Horticultural Associates, Inc., in cooperation with Amfac® Garden Products.

Executive Producer: Richard Ray
Contributing Author: Claire Barrett
Consultants: Fred Galle, Ralph Miller, Carl A. Totemeier, Richard Turner, Joseph A. Witt
Photography: Michael Landis
Art Director: Richard Baker
Book Design: Judith Hemmerich
Associate Editors: Michael MacCaskey, Lance Walheim
Research Editor: Randy Peterson
Copy Editors: Greg Boucher, Miriam Boucher
Production Editor: Kathleen Parker
Book Production: Lingke Moeis
Illustrations: Charles Hoeppner, Roy Jones
Typography: Linda Encinas
Additional Photography: William Aplin, Susan A. Roth
Cover Photo: Michael Landis
Acknowledgements: Jim Gibbons, Horticulturist, San Diego Wild Animal Park, Escondido, CA; Jean Michels, Garden Designer, St. Helena, CA; Los Angeles Arboretum; Henry Koide, Presidio Garden Center, San Diego, CA.

Lath house shown on cover designed by William Turnbull.

For Western Publishing Company, Inc.:
Editorial Director: Jonathan P. Latimer
Senior Editor: Susan A. Roth
Copy Editor: Karen Stray Nolting

Golden Press • New York
Western Publishing Company, Inc.
Racine, Wisconsin

Library of Congress Catalog Card Number 82-81413
Golden® and Golden Press® are trademarks of Western Publishing Company, Inc.
ISBN 0-307-46625-6

Top-Rated Vines

This book is designed to help you choose perennial vines for a variety of landscape uses. The encyclopedia section will help you select the best vine for a particular situation, and the planting and care information will assist you in successfully growing the vines you choose.

Top-Rated Vines describes only the best vines—ones that were selected by gardening experts as being proven performers. These vines are readily available at local garden centers.

Vines in your landscape: These graceful plants can add an exciting new dimension to a landscape. Vines take up practically no ground space, but can provide a display of greenery or colorful flowers just about anywhere. Many species flower brilliantly or fill the garden air with sweet fragrance. Others are prized for their delicate foliage that provides a softening tracery on walls and fences. Some vines make excellent ground covers. The landscape section in this book, starting on page 9, is full of ideas to help you use vines effectively around your home.

Plant names: Common names are so variable they cannot be used for accurate plant identification. The name cross-reference guide on page 63 matches the most widely used common names for each vine with its botanical name.

Plants adapted to your region: The charts on pages 6 and 7 are a general guide to top-rated vines for your growing region. Before making a final choice, read the complete description of the plant in the encyclopedia section.

Climbing hydrangea *(Hydrangea anomala)* blankets bare walls with greenery in spring and summer; produces showy white blooms in late spring.

Chinese jasmine *(Jasminum sp.)*

Blood-red trumpet vine *(Distictis sp.)*

Fatshedera *(x Fatshedera lizei)*

Clematis *(Clematis sp.)*

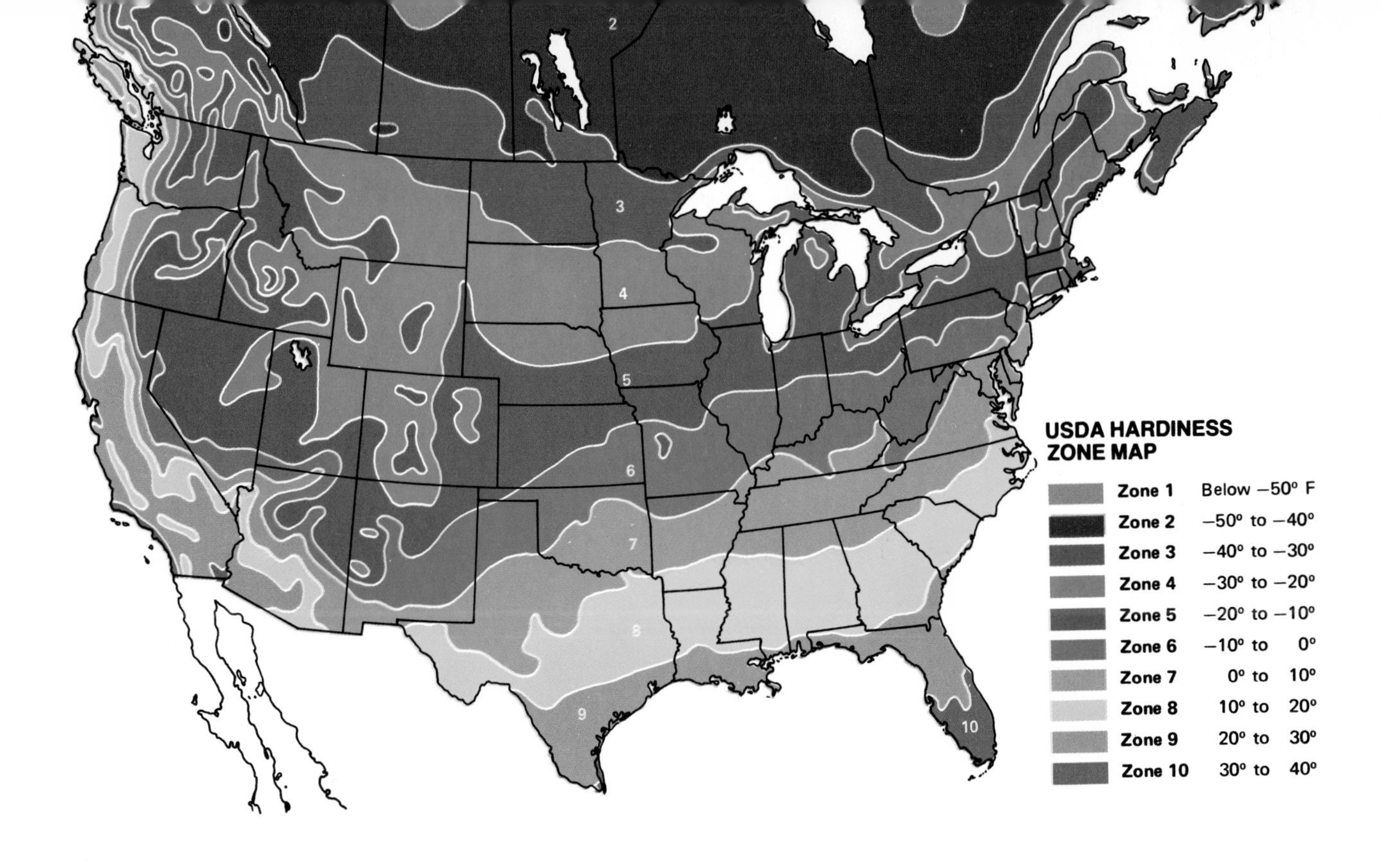

Climates for Vines

The plant hardiness map shows the average low temperatures throughout the United States and Southern Canada. It divides North America into 10 zones with the average minimum temperature of each zone differing by 10 degrees Fahrenheit. All vines in this book are identified in the following charts and in the encyclopedia by the zones where they are considered to be top-rated. Use the map to find your climate zone so you can select appropriate plants for your garden.

As every gardener learns, cold hardiness is only one factor of a plant's adaptation. A plant's ability to do well in a certain location depends on unique combinations of soil type, wind, rainfall, length and time of cold, humidity, summer temperatures, and temperatures in relation to humidity. For example, American and European grape varieties are prone to disease problems in the southern United States because of the high humidity. However, the native muscadine grape is widely used in southern states because it thrives in hot, humid conditions.

Note that in listing zone numbers, a plant's adaptation to climates is indicated not only by the lowest temperatures but also by its ability to grow in warmer climates at the other end of the spectrum. *Clematis x jackmanii* is listed in Zones 5 to 10, while *Euonymus fortunei* is best adapted to Zones 4 to 8.

Some fruiting plants need a specific cold period to stimulate flowering and fruiting. Most varieties of kiwi have a chilling requirement of 600 to 800 hours at temperatures below 45°F. This factor must be considered in addition to the USDA hardiness zones, if you expect your kiwi vine to be productive.

The USDA hardiness zone map does not take other climate factors into consideration. To give you additional information, we have broken down the United States into 10 climate regions. The map and charts on the following pages show both the hardiness zone and regional adaptation. For a plant to be adapted to your area, it should be recommended for your USDA hardiness zone and your climate region.

USDA Zones 8 to 10 are particularly complex in the western United States. Many plants with a southern range of Zone 8 can also be grown in Zones 9 and 10 in the West. In these cases, it is best to follow regional recommendations.

The climates around your home: Another aspect of climate important in selecting vines is microclimate. Microclimates are the small climates around your home that differ slightly from the general climate of your area. The northern side of your property, which is probably partially shaded most of the day by your house, is a cold microclimate. The southern side of your home, which, unless shaded by trees, receives hot sun almost all day, is a warm microclimate. A good way to

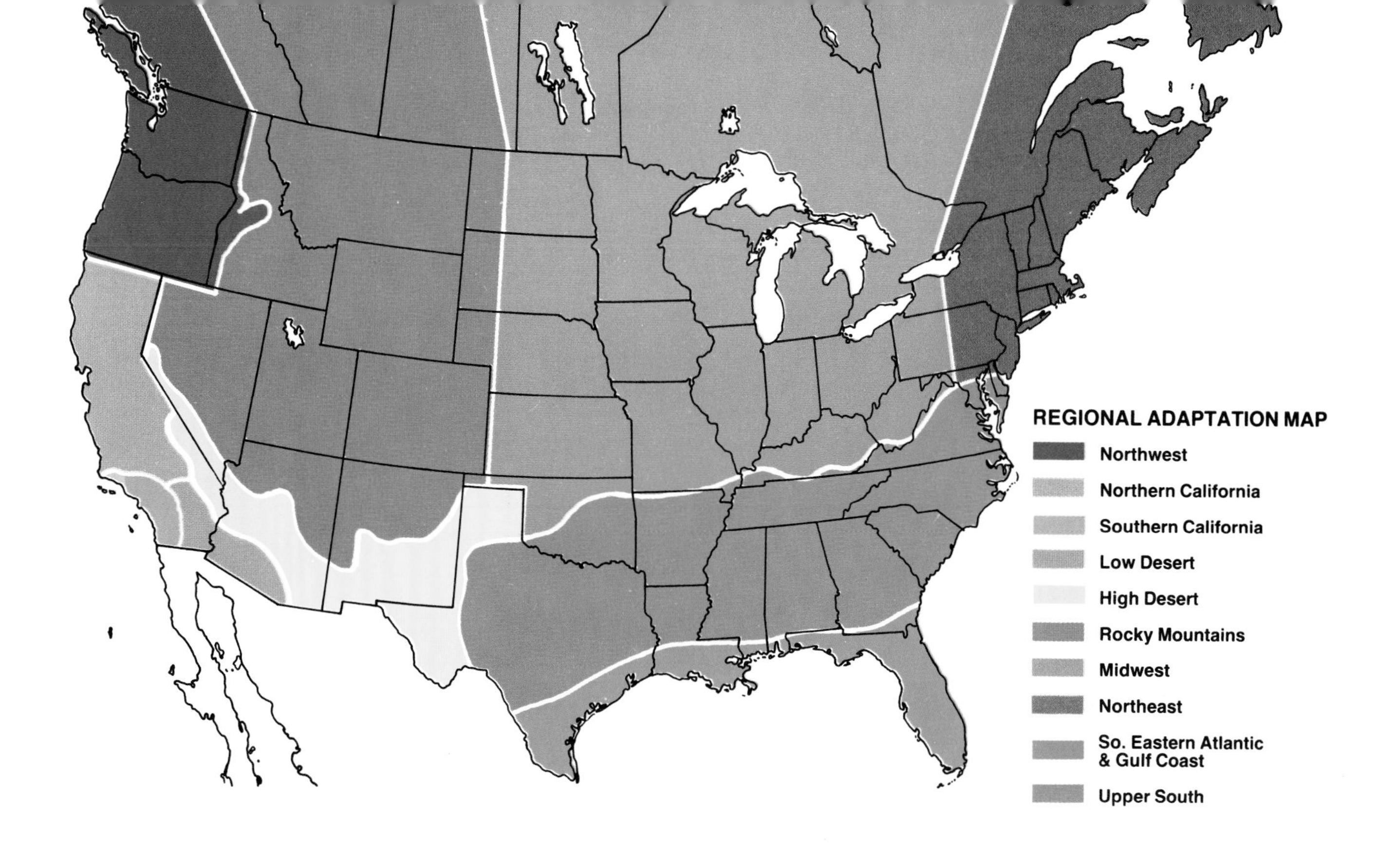

become aware of microclimates is by making a site plan. (See page 10.)

Plants that are borderline hardy for your area may do well if you take protective measures such as providing wind or snow shelters and making use of your property's warm microclimates. Protected plants can often be grown successfully in the next colder zone.

Information about regional climates:

Northwest: The cool moist climates typified by the cities of Portland and Seattle are strongly influenced by the Pacific Ocean. Soils are generally acid. High elevation areas east of the Cascade Mountain Range begin to resemble the Rocky Mountain region.

Northern California: A diverse climate region influenced by proximity to the Pacific Ocean. Inland areas have warm summers and cool winters. Coastal areas are milder in summer and winter.

Southern California: High summer temperatures, mild winters, and low annual rainfall characterize this area. It differs greatly from areas along the Gulf Coast that are in the same USDA Zones. Soils are often alkaline.

Low Desert: Typified by the cities of Palm Springs, California, and Phoenix and Tucson, Arizona. Soils are often alkaline. Very hot summers with strong winds and high light intensity are common. Winters are mild, low temperatures depend on the elevation.

High Desert: Represents a wide range of mostly high elevation areas with hot summers, cold winters, and low annual rainfall. Soils are often alkaline.

Rocky Mountains: Generally high elevation areas with abundant winter snowfall and short summers. Lower elevation areas such as Denver, Colorado, and Salt Lake City, Utah, can grow the widest range of plant material.

Midwest: Includes the dry, windy climates of the Great Plains and moister areas around the Great Lakes. Climates change drastically over short distances around the Great Lakes because of their proximity to water.

Northeast: Winters here are generally milder than in the Midwest due to the moderating effect of the Atlantic Ocean. However, high elevation areas can be very cold. Soils are typically acid.

Southeastern Atlantic and Gulf Coast: A narrow strip of land with mild winters and hot, humid summers. Annual rainfall is high and is dispersed evenly throughout the year.

Upper South: A zone made up of many different climates influenced by elevation, latitude, and proximity to the Atlantic Ocean. Its northern, southern, and eastern boundaries are a transition to adjacent regions.

Herald's-trumpet *(Beaumontia grandiflora)* bears spectacular lilylike blooms from spring into summer. Use as a fence or patio cover, espaliered, or pruned as a mounding shrub.

Regional Adaptation

PLANT NAME	ZONES	NORTHWEST	NORTHERN CALIFORNIA	SOUTHERN CALIFORNIA	LOW DESERT	HIGH DESERT	ROCKY MOUNTAINS	MIDWEST	NORTHEAST	SO. EASTERN ATLANTIC & GULF COAST	UPPER SOUTH
Actinidia chinensis	8-10	■	■	■						■	■
Antigonon leptopus	8-10			■	■					■	
Beaumontia grandiflora	10			■	■					■	
Bougainvillea sp.	9-10		■	■	■					■	
Campsis grandiflora	7-8		■	■	■	■					■
Campsis radicans	4-8	■	■	■	■	■	■	■	■		■
Campsis x tagliabuana 'Madame Galen'	4-8	■	■	■	■	■	■	■	■		■
Celastrus orbiculatus	5-9	■	■				■	■	■		■
Celastrus scandens	3-9	■	■				■	■	■		■
Clematis armandii	8-10	■	■	■	■					■	■
Clematis x jackmanii	5-10	■	■	■	■		■	■	■	■	■
Clematis texensis	4-10	■	■	■	■	■	■	■	■	■	■
Clytostoma callistegioides	9-10		■	■	■					■	
Distictis buccinatoria	9-10		■	■						■	
Distictis laxiflora	9-10		■	■						■	
Euonymus fortunei	4-8	■	■		■	■		■	■		■
x Fatshedera lizei	9-10	■	■	■	■					■	
Ficus pumila	9-10		■	■	■	■				■	■
Gelsemium sempervirens	7-10		■	■	■	■				■	■
Hedera canariensis	8-10		■	■	■					■	■
Hedera helix	5-10	■	■	■	■	■	■	■	■	■	■

Clematis *(Clematis sp.)* varieties are widely adapted and offer a large selection of flower shapes, sizes, colors, and blooming season. All are stunning in the landscape.

Regional Adaptation

PLANT NAME	ZONES	NORTHWEST	NORTHERN CALIFORNIA	SOUTHERN CALIFORNIA	LOW DESERT	HIGH DESERT	ROCKY MOUNTAINS	MIDWEST	NORTHEAST	SO. EASTERN ATLANTIC & GULF COAST	UPPER SOUTH
Hibbertia scandens	10			■						■	
Hydrangea anomala	5-9	■	■	■	■	■	■	■	■	■	■
Jasminum nitidum	10			■	■					■	
Jasminum polyanthum	8-10		■	■	■					■	■
Lonicera hildebrandiana	9-10		■	■						■	
Lonicera japonica	4-10	■	■	■	■	■	■	■	■	■	■
Lonicera sempervirens	4-10	■	■	■	■	■	■	■	■	■	■
Parthenocissus sp.	4-10	■	■	■	■	■	■	■	■	■	■
Passiflora x alatocaerulea	9-10		■	■	■					■	■
Passiflora caerulea	9-10	■	■	■	■					■	■
Passiflora edulis	9-10		■	■	■					■	
Polygonum aubertii	5-10	■	■	■	■	■	■	■	■	■	■
Rhoicissus capensis	10		■	■						■	
Rosa hybrids	5-10	■	■	■	■	■	■	■	■	■	■
Tecomaria capensis	9-10		■	■	■					■	
Trachelospermum asiaticum	7-10		■	■	■					■	■
Trachelospermum jasminoides	8-10		■	■	■					■	■
Vitis labrusca	6-10	■	■	■			■	■	■		■
Vitis rotundifolia	8-10									■	■
Vitis vinifera	7-10	■	■	■		■					
Wisteria floribunda	5-9	■	■	■	■	■	■	■	■	■	■
Wisteria sinensis	5-9	■	■	■	■	■	■	■	■	■	■

Using Vines in Your Garden

Vines are problem solvers in the landscape. They can fit into the smallest space or cover the largest area. Grown on a trellis they can block an unpleasant view; grown on the ground they can quickly cover bare spots. Where plants are needed to soften the stark side of a house or decorate a bare fence, but where there's no room for shrubs, a vine can provide a show of flowers or foliage and use almost no ground space.

While a complete lesson in landscaping with vines is beyond the scope of this book, a few examples of how you can use them will show their versatility.

LANDSCAPE USES

Accent: A climbing rose or clematis can turn a nondescript post or fence into a garden focal point.

Color and fragrance: Vines can place flower color and fragrance right where you want it—high or low, to look up into, or down upon. Sweet-scented, spectacularly colored blossoms of honeysuckle or jasmine can be grown where you can appreciate them most.

Containers: Many vines are ideal for growing in hanging containers. Most of these, such as bougainvillea and star jasmine, will drape and cascade over the edges of pots and hanging baskets.

Filler: Vines can grow in areas without needing much space. Along narrow sides of houses they can add greenery on a fence or wall without blocking traffic.

Ground covers: Vines don't have to climb, they can trail along the ground, rooting as they go. Bare ground can be quickly dressed up with a suitable vine.

Creeping fig *(Ficus pumila)* covers walls with dense, fine-textured, evergreen foliage. Clings tightly; needs little space.

Herald's-trumpet *(Beaumontia sp.)*

Cape honeysuckle *(Tecomaria sp.)*

Boston ivy *(Parthenocissus sp.)*

Clematis *(Clematis sp.)*

Grapes *(Vitis sp.)* are dual-purpose vines; they provide cooling shade and edible fruit.

Chinese jasmine *(Jasminum polyanthum)* makes a light-textured cover for beams and posts; fragrant blossoms scent the garden for months.

Privacy: Trained over a fence or trellis, fast-growing vines such as Virginia creeper form effective privacy screens faster than many shrubs.

Shade: Trained over an arbor or pergola, fast-growing vines such as grape or wisteria can shade a patio much more quickly than a tree.

Softening: Vines can soften bright or blank walls with foliage and flowers. They can add contour to a jutting extension or turn a utilitarian fence into an ornamental asset.

Specimen: Specimen plants are eye-catching plants that are set apart in the landscape. Some vines, such as wisteria, can be trained into a tree or shrub form, others can command attention when trained into a formal-looking espalier.

SITE PLAN

One way to better understand how plants can solve landscape problems is to develop a site plan. A site plan is a sketch or diagram, drawn to scale, of your house and yard. It shows the location of doors, windows, and rooms, and existing plants, decks or patios—anything that will affect your planting. It will also note other physical aspects of your property, such as good and bad views from both indoors and out, prevailing winds, low spots and slopes, paths of air circulation, and sun patterns.

Done properly, a site plan takes a good deal of time and observation to prepare. You will need to note which areas are sunny in summer, shady in winter, and vice versa, as well as understand wind changes

Sketching a site plan of your property, similar to the example shown below, helps you identify your landscape needs. Once you note which views need to be blocked or preserved, where shade is needed, areas of poor soil or bad drainage, and paths of movement, you can begin to choose plants that meet your specific landscape requirements.

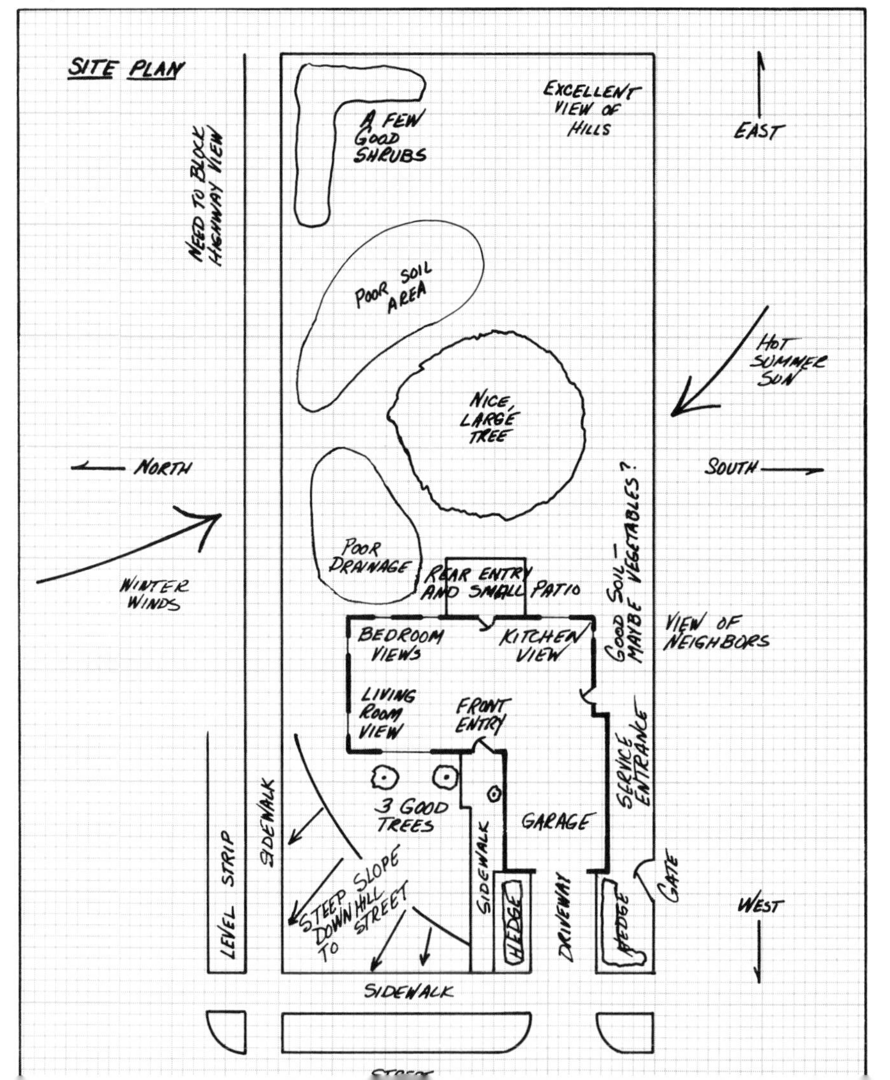

Deciduous flowering vines and trees save energy. Their shade blocks hot sun in summer, keeping your house cool and reducing air conditioning costs. In winter their bare branches let sunlight through, warming your house and lowering heating costs.

from season to season. These observations will help you choose the right vine for a particular spot.

PLANT CHARACTERISTICS

Evergreen or deciduous: Do you want the vine to retain its leaves year-round? Vines used to screen unpleasant views should do so the entire year. Those meant to provide cooling summer shade could also let warm sun through in cooler months if they are deciduous, dropping their leaves in fall.

Blossoms: Some of the world's most spectacular flowering plants are vines. When choosing a flowering vine, bloom season and flower color are obviously important. Though most flowering vines bloom in spring, there are ones that bloom in summer and some that scatter bloom throughout the year.

Choose flower colors with a painter's eye. Be sure they complement or blend with other plants that are in bloom at the same time. Also keep the color of your house in mind when choosing flower colors. For instance, setting a white climbing rose beside a white house would lessen the impact of the flowers, while the same climbing rose would be nicely highlighted against a dark-colored house.

Flower colors can have strikingly different effects on the landscape. White is a natural choice to lighten up shaded areas or to cool hot spots. Blue is also a cool, soothing color. Yellows and reds are generally vibrant, warm colors that can make a cool spot seem warm—or a hot area even hotter.

Habit: Consider how large an area a vine will cover when it is full grown and how it will affect the surrounding landscape. The texture of a vine is also important. The size and shape of leaves, and whether the flowers, if any, are bold- or fine-textured, will determine how a vine blends with its background and the surrounding landscape. Small-leaved varieties of English ivy look especially nice against brick. More vigorous-growing, woody vines appear to best advantage on large arbors made of thick beams.

Vines use different methods to attach themselves to surfaces and climb. Ones such as wisteria, which have twining stems, require a post, trellis, arbor, wires, string, or similar support to wind around. Vines such as grapes, which climb with coiling tendrils, also need support, and usually a small or narrow lattice or wire is adequate.

Other vines, such as English ivy, climb by clinging rootlets or suction cups and ascend walls, fences, and tree trunks without assistance. However, once attached they may be very difficult to remove and can actually damage the surface they cling to. Shingles, mortar and red brick may be damaged by the "holdfasts", especially if you attempt to remove the vines. To help avoid the problem, clinging vines should be cut back at ground level and allowed to die before you remove them.

Still other vines, including bougainvillea and climbing roses, must be tied to a trellis or support. Left on their own, they will become sprawling, shrublike plants.

Rate of Growth: If you want an immediate effect, choose fast-growing vines. But beware. Some of the fastest-growing vines keep up their rampant growth even after they have achieved the effect you want. If you don't choose the vine carefully, it may grow into areas where it isn't wanted, necessitating extra pruning and labor. Some vines, if allowed to get out of control, can strangle trees or smaller plants.

Wisteria *(Wisteria sp.)* is a widely adapted vine. Its light-green foliage is handsome in the landscape long after its spectacular spring bloom is gone.

Chinese jasmine *(Jasminum polyanthum)* quickly climbs a trellis; scents the air with fragrant flowers in spring.

Special features: Once you realize what kind of vine you need, look for additional ornamental bonuses. Fall foliage color, brightly colored fruit, or colorful new growth can make a vine a beautiful addition to the garden for many months of the year.

Maintenance: Certain vines require less pruning, watering, or spraying than others. See page 62 to see how much care a given vine requires. Also, fruit-bearing vines can require a yearly cleanup if the fruit is not used.

SUPPORT FOR VINES

The type of support you need to provide for a vine depends upon how the vine climbs. Vines can be categorized into two broad groups—clinging and non-clinging—based on their manner of climbing.

Clinging vines: Clinging vines, typified by trumpet vine, wintercreeper, creeping fig, climbing hydrangea, and English ivy, attach themselves to nearly any rough surface by rootlets that form on their stems. Boston ivy, also a tenacious clinger, produces clusters of small suction cups that will adhere to almost any rough- or smooth-textured surface.

Clinging vines are at their best planted against masonry or stone, where they soften the appearance of a blank wall with a tracery of stems and foliage. However, their rootlets and suction cups can sometimes do damage. If the walls are old and in poor condition, the rootlets can make the mortar crumble. New walls can also be damaged if the mortar is weak because too much sand was used in proportion to cement. If the mortar is recessed between the bricks—do this when building a new wall with a convex jointing tool—the rootlets will cling to the bricks and ignore the mortar.

On wood or shingle walls, or on brick walls where vines might damage the mortar, grow clinging vines on a trellis placed six inches away from the building's surface. Clingers will also ascend wood fences, tree trunks, and even chain link fences.

Non-clinging vines: Vines that grow by coiling tendrils or twining stems are called non-clinging. They need some kind of support they can wrap around. For ones with tendrils this means a trellis or fence with a lattice of supporting pieces that are no more than an inch in diameter and fairly close together. A trellis, chain link fence, or latticework pergola make good supports.

Vines that grow by twining or coiling stems can grow on sturdier supports such as posts and split-rail or picket fences. Use them to accent a lamppost, mailbox, or porch railing as well as to decorate trellises and arbors.

Whatever kind of support you use, be sure it is sturdy enough to hold the weight of a mature vine. Old grape and wisteria vines have immense, heavy branches that need a strong trellis or arbor to hold them up.

As with clinging vines, twining vines can damage buildings. Robust twiners can wrap their strong stems around a tree trunk and eventually strangle the tree. Bittersweet and wisteria are notorious for this kind of destructive behavior. Twiners have also been known to damage shingles when in search for something to twine around. Their long stems sometimes grow up behind wood shingles, prying them off the building. It's best to keep rampant twiners confined to a trellis that is six inches away from the wall if you plan to grow them against the house.

Trellises: Nearly all garden centers offer a good selection of trellises in a choice of sizes and finishes. It isn't difficult however to build your own trellis. You can design a trellis that will blend with your home's architecture so that it becomes a visual extension of your home. Use pressure-treated wood or redwood or cedar so the trellis will withstand the elements.

One trick when putting up a trellis, whether you purchase it or build it yourself, is to attach it to the wall with hinges at the bottom and with hooks at the top. Secured this way, the trellis together with the vines can be easily moved away from the wall without harming the plants when it's time to paint.

If a trellis seems out of keeping with your home's architecture, there are less conspicuous ways to get a vine to grow up a wall. Wire cables attached to a masonry or stone wall by expansion bolts and tightened with turnbuckles are excellent for holding heavy vines such as wisteria. One method is to space the cables 2 to 4 feet apart in overlapping horizontal and vertical rows. The vines can be woven through the wires until they begin to twine or cling.

Cables may also be arranged in decorative patterns to create an espalier. Fan shapes or garlands are especially popular.

Wires should be rustproof. Copper ones are best—they will weather to an unobtrusive brown color. Wire covered with dark weatherproof plastic, the kind used in electrical work, is also good.

Maintaining supports: Check wood supports annually for signs of decay so any necessary repairs can be made quickly and easily. Replace damaged or decayed portions by bolting a new anchor to the upright. Pressure-treated lumber is decay-resistant and is excellent for trellises and other outdoor uses. Turnbuckles should also be tightened occasionally to maintain adequate cable tension.

SELECTION AID

The lists that follow will help you choose the right vine. They describe vines that solve problems, have specific attractions, or fit into difficult climate conditions.

Use these lists as an introduction to the descriptions of vines in the plant encyclopedia section. Do not decide on any vine until you have read its complete description. If a vine is listed without a specific species, such as *Lonicera sp.*, it means there are several species to choose from. You must go to the individual plant description for information needed to make a valid choice.

How Vines Climb

Boston ivy *(Parthenocissus tricuspidata)* clings with disc-like suction cups to rough- or smooth-textured surfaces.

English ivy *(Hedera helix)* is a clinging vine that adheres to rough surfaces with tiny rootlets that grow from the stems.

A non-clinging vine, star jasmine *(Trachelospermum jasminoides)* climbs by weaving its stems through a lattice.

Other non-clinging vines such as grape *(Vitis sp.)* climb by grasping onto wires or lattices with tightly coiling tendrils.

Jackman clematis *(Clematis x jackmanii)*

Carolina jessamine *(Gelsemium sp.)*

Hybrid passionflower *(Passiflora sp.)*

Vine Landscape Use Lists

Blue to Purple Flowers

		Zones
Bougainvillea sp.	Bougainvillea	9-10
Clematis x jackmanii	Jackman Clematis	5-10
Clytostoma callistegioides	Violet Trumpet Vine	9-10
Distictis laxiflora	Vanilla Trumpet Vine	9-10
Passiflora sp.	Passionflower	9-10
Wisteria sp.	Wisteria	5-9

Pink to Red Flowers

		Zones
Antigonon leptopus	Coral Vine	8-10
Bougainvillea sp.	Bougainvillea	9-10
Campsis sp.	Trumpet Creeper	4-8
Clematis sp.	Clematis	4-10
Distictis buccinatoria	Blood-Red Trumpet Vine	9-10
Lonicera sempervirens	Trumpet Honeysuckle	4-10
Passiflora sp.	Passionflower	9-10
Rosa hybrids	Climbing Rose	5-10
Tecomaria capensis	Cape Honeysuckle	9-10
Wisteria sp.	Wisteria	5-9

Yellow Flowers

		Zones
Bougainvillea sp.	Bougainvillea	9-10
Gelsemium sempervirens	Carolina Yellow Jessamine	7-10
Hibbertia scandens	Gold Guinea Plant	10
Jasminum sp.	Jasmine	8-10
Lonicera sp.	Honeysuckle	4-10
Rosa hybrids	Climbing Rose	5-10
Tecomaria capensis	Cape Honeysuckle	9-10
Trachelospermum asiaticum	Yellow Star Jasmine	7-10

White Flowers

		Zones
Actinidia chinensis	Kiwi	8-10
Antigonon leptopus	Coral Vine	8-10
Beaumontia grandiflora	Herald's-Trumpet	10
Bougainvillea sp.	Bougainvillea	9-10
Celastrus sp.	Bittersweet	3-9
Clematis armandii	Evergreen Clematis	8-10
x Fatshedera lizei	Fatshedera	9-10
Hydrangea anomala	Climbing Hydrangea	5-9
Jasminum sp.	Jasmine	8-10
Lonicera sp.	Honeysuckle	4-10
Passiflora sp.	Passionflower	9-10
Polygonum aubertii	Silver Lace Vine	5-10
Rosa hybrids	Climbing Rose	5-10
Trachelospermum jasminoides	Star Jasmine	8-10
Wisteria sp.	Wisteria	5-9

Fragrant Flowers

		Zones
Actinidia chinensis	Kiwi	7-10
Beaumontia grandiflora	Herald's-Trumpet	10
Clematis armandii	Evergreen Clematis	8-10
Distictis laxiflora	Vanilla Trumpet Vine	9-10
Gelsemium sempervirens	Carolina Yellow Jessamine	7-10
Jasminum sp.	Jasmine	8-10
Lonicera sp.	Honeysuckle	4-10
Passiflora x alatocaerulea	Hybrid Passionflower	9-10
Rosa hybrids	Climbing Rose	5-10
Trachelospermum sp.	Star Jasmine	7-10
Wisteria sp.	Wisteria	5-9

Spring Bloom

		Zones
Actinidia chinensis	Kiwi	8-10
Beaumontia grandiflora	Herald's-Trumpet	10
Bougainvillea sp.	Bougainvillea	9-10
Clematis armandii	Evergreen Clematis	8-10
Clytostoma callistegioides	Violet Trumpet Vine	9-10
Distictis sp.	Trumpet Vine	9-10
Gelsemium sempervirens	Carolina Yellow Jessamine	7-10
Hibbertia scandens	Gold Guinea Plant	10
Jasminum sp.	Jasmine	8-10
Rosa hybrids	Climbing Rose	5-10
Trachelospermum sp.	Star Jasmine	7-10
Wisteria sp.	Wisteria	5-9

Boston ivy *(Parthenocissus sp.)*

Trumpet vine *(Distictis sp.)*

Cape honeysuckle *(Tecomaria sp.)*

Interesting Fruits

These vines produce both flowers and interesting fruit. Those vines marked with an * bear edible fruit.

		Zones
*Actinidia chinensis**	Kiwi	8-10
Celastrus sp.	Bittersweet	3-9
Clematis sp.	Clematis	4-10
Lonicera sempervirens	Trumpet Honeysuckle	4-10
Parthenocissus sp.	Boston Ivy, Virginia Creeper	4-10
*Passiflora edulis**	Purple Granadilla	9-10
Rhoicissus capensis	Cape Grape	10
*Vitis sp.**	Grape	6-10

Colorful Foliage

These vines add color to the garden with either multicolored leaves or brilliant autumn foliage.

		Zones
Celastrus sp.	Bittersweet	3-9
Euonymus fortunei	Wintercreeper	4-8
Hedera helix 'Aureo-variegata'	Yellow-Variegated English Ivy	5-10
Hedera helix 'Gold Heart'	Gold Heart English Ivy	5-10
Lonicera japonica 'Aureo-reticulata'	Gold-Net Honeysuckle	4-10
Parthenocissus sp.	Boston Ivy, Virginia Creeper	4-10
Rhoicissus capensis	Cape Grape	10
Trachelospermum jasminoides 'Variegatum'	Variegated Star Jasmine	8-10
Vitis sp.	Grape	6-10

Color in More Than One Season

These vines make planning for year-round color in the landscape easier. Flowers extending across the seasons and bright-colored foliage or fruit can create continuous visual interest.

		Zones
Actinidia chinensis	Kiwi	8-10
Antigonon leptopus	Coral Vine	8-10
Beaumontia grandiflora	Herald's-Trumpet	10
Bougainvillea sp.	Bougainvillea	9-10
Celastrus sp.	Bittersweet	3-9
Clematis sp.	Clematis	4-10
Clytostoma callistegioides	Violet Trumpet Vine	9-10
Distictis sp.	Trumpet Vine	9-10
Euonymus fortunei	Wintercreeper	4-8
Gelsemium sempervirens	Carolina Yellow Jessamine	7-10
Hedera helix 'Aureo-variegata'	Yellow-Variegated English Ivy	5-10
Hedera helix 'Gold Heart'	Gold Heart English Ivy	5-10
Hibbertia scandens	Gold Guinea Plant	10
Jasminum sp.	Jasmine	8-10
Lonicera sempervirens	Trumpet Honeysuckle	4-10
Parthenocissus sp.	Boston Ivy, Virginia Creeper	4-10
Passiflora edulis	Purple Granadilla	9-10
Polygonum aubertii	Silver Lace Vine	5-10
Rosa hybrids	Climbing Rose	5-10
Tecomaria capensis	Cape Honeysuckle	9-10
Vitis sp.	Grape	6-10

Summer Bloom

		Zones
Antigonon leptopus	Coral Vine	8-10
Beaumontia grandiflora	Herald's-Trumpet	10
Bougainvillea sp.	Bougainvillea	9-10
Campsis sp.	Trumpet Creeper	4-8
Clematis sp.	Clematis	4-10
Clytostoma callistegioides	Violet Trumpet Vine	9-10
Distictis sp.	Trumpet Vine	9-10
Hibbertia scandens	Gold Guinea Plant	10
Hydrangea anomala	Climbing Hydrangea	5-9
Jasminum sp.	Jasmine	8-10
Lonicera sp.	Honeysuckle	4-10
Passiflora sp.	Passionflower	9-10
Polygonum aubertii	Silver Lace Vine	5-10
Rosa hybrids	Climbing Rose	5-10
Tecomaria capensis	Cape Honeysuckle	9-10

Fall Bloom

Fall-blooming vines add exciting color when few other plants are in bloom. Use them with earlier flowering vines for nearly year-long color in the garden.

		Zones
Antigonon leptopus	Coral Vine	8-10
Bougainvillea sp.	Bougainvillea	9-10
Clematis sp.	Clematis	4-10
Clytostoma callistegioides	Violet Trumpet Vine	9-10
Distictis sp.	Trumpet Vine	9-10
x Fatshedera lizei	Fatshedera	9-10
Hibbertia scandens	Gold Guinea Plant	10
Polygonum aubertii	Silver Lace Vine	5-10
Rosa hybrids	Climbing Rose	5-10
Tecomaria capensis	Cape Honeysuckle	9-10

Honeysuckle *(Lonicera sp.)*

Vigorous, Fast-Growers

When a fast shade cover is desired or an unsightly view needs screening, these are the vines that can do the job. They can give a young landscape a mature look in just a few years.

Botanical Name	Common Name	Zones
Actinidia chinensis	Kiwi	8-10
Antigonon leptopus	Coral Vine	8-10
Beaumontia grandiflora	Herald's-Trumpet	10
Bougainvillea sp.	Bougainvillea	9-10
Campsis sp.	Trumpet Creeper	4-8
Celastrus sp.	Bittersweet	3-9
Clematis sp.	Clematis	4-10
Clytostoma callistegioides	Violet Trumpet Vine	9-10
Distictis sp.	Trumpet Vine	9-10
Ficus pumila	Creeping Fig	9-10
Hedera helix	English Ivy	5-10
Hibbertia scandens	Gold Guinea Plant	10
Hydrangea anomala	Climbing Hydrangea	5-9
Jasminum polyanthum	Chinese Jasmine	8-10
Lonicera sp.	Honeysuckle	4-10
Parthenocissus sp.	Boston Ivy, Virginia Creeper	4-10
Passiflora sp.	Passionflower	9-10
Polygonum aubertii	Silver Lace Vine	5-10
Rosa hybrids	Climbing Rose	5-10
Tecomaria capensis	Cape Honeysuckle	9-10
Trachelospermum sp.	Star Jasmine	7-10
Vitis sp.	Grape	6-10
Wisteria sp.	Wisteria	5-9

Cape honeysuckle *(Tecomaria sp.)*

Windy Sites

Harsh winds can dry out leaves or cause them to tear. High winds can pull branches of upright vines off their supports. The vines listed below withstand windy conditions because they have tough leaves and flexible branches, and attach securely to their supports.

Botanical Name	Common Name	Zones
Celastrus sp.	Bittersweet	3-9
Clytostoma callistegioides	Violet Trumpet Vine	9-10
Distictis sp.	Trumpet Vine	9-10
Euonymus fortunei	Wintercreeper	4-8
Ficus pumila	Creeping Fig	9-10
Gelsemium sempervirens	Carolina Yellow Jessamine	7-10
Hydrangea anomala	Climbing Hydrangea	5-9
Parthenocissus sp.	Boston Ivy, Virginia Creeper	4-10
Polygonum aubertii	Silver Lace Vine	5-10
Tecomaria capensis	Cape Honeysuckle	9-10
Trachelospermum sp.	Star Jasmine	7-10

Star jasmine *(Trachelospermum sp.)*

Ground Covers

These are double-duty plants in the landscape, serving equally well as ground covers or upright vines. The fast growers make excellent alternatives to slow-establishing ground covers or grass lawns. More restrained growers form neat carpets for small areas.

Many of the vines will root along their stems to serve as soil stabilizers on steep slopes.

Botanical Name	Common Name	Zones
Antigonon leptopus	Coral Vine	8-10
Bougainvillea sp.	Bougainvillea	9-10
Celastrus sp.	Bittersweet	3-9
Clematis sp.	Clematis	4-10
Euonymus fortunei	Wintercreeper	4-8
x Fatshedera lizei	Fatshedera	9-10
Gelsemium sempervirens	Carolina Yellow Jessamine	7-10
Hedera helix	English Ivy	5-10
Hibbertia scandens	Gold Guinea Plant	10
Jasminum sp.	Jasmine	8-10
Lonicera sp.	Honeysuckle	4-10
Parthenocissus sp.	Boston Ivy, Virginia Creeper	4-10
Passiflora caerulea	Blue Passionflower	9-10
Rhoicissus capensis	Cape Grape	10
Rosa hybrids	Climbing Rose	5-10
Tecomaria capensis	Cape Honeysuckle	9-10
Trachelospermum sp.	Star Jasmine	7-10

Wintercreeper *(Euonymus fortunei)*

Clematis *(Clematis sp.)*

Boston ivy *(Parthenocissus sp.)*

Shady Areas

Shady spots can be problem spots in the landscape. The following vines are problem-solvers. Give early afternoon exposures or dappled light for plants requiring partial shade.

		Zones
Actinidia chinensis	Kiwi	8-10
Celastrus sp.	Bittersweet	3-9
Clematis sp.	Clematis	4-10
Clytostoma callistegioides	Violet Trumpet Vine	9-10
Distictis sp.	Trumpet Vine	9-10
Euonymus fortunei	Wintercreeper	4-8
x Fatshedera lizei	Fatshedera	9-10
Ficus pumila	Creeping Fig	9-10
Gelsemium sempervirens	Carolina Yellow Jessamine	7-10
Hedera helix	English Ivy	5-10
Hibbertia scandens	Gold Guinea Plant	10
Hydrangea anomala	Climbing Hydrangea	5-9
Jasminum sp.	Jasmine	8-10
Lonicera sp.	Honeysuckle	4-10
Parthenocissus sp.	Boston Ivy, Virginia Creeper	4-10
Polygonum aubertii	Silver Lace Vine	5-10
Rhoicissus capensis	Cape Grape	10
Tecomaria capensis	Cape Honeysuckle	9-10
Trachelospermum sp.	Star Jasmine	7-10
Wisteria sp.	Wisteria	5-9

Twining Vines

The branches of these vines will twist, circle, and weave themselves through an open fence, wire trellis, or post to form upright vines.

		Zones
Actinidia chinensis	Kiwi	8-10
Beaumontia grandiflora	Herald's-Trumpet	10
Bougainvillea sp.	Bougainvillea	9-10
Celastrus sp.	Bittersweet	3-9
Clematis sp.	Clematis	4-10
Gelsemium sempervirens	Carolina Yellow Jessamine	7-10
Hibbertia scandens	Gold Guinea Plant	10
Jasminum sp.	Jasmine	8-10
Lonicera sp.	Honeysuckle	4-10
Polygonum aubertii	Silver Lace Vine	5-10
Tecomaria capensis	Cape Honeysuckle	9-10
Vitis sp.	Grape	6-10
Wisteria sp.	Wisteria	5-9

Vines with Tendrils

Tendrils are slender stalks that form on branches, stems, or the ends of flower and leaf stalks. They twist and curl on making contact with a surface to hold the vine in place. Young plants may need tying before tendrils are formed, but once established are self-supporting vines.

		Zones
Antigonon leptopus	Coral Vine	8-10
Clematis sp.	Clematis	4-10
Clytostoma callistegioides	Violet Trumpet Vine	9-10
Distictis sp.	Trumpet Vine	9-10
Parthenocissus sp.	Boston Ivy, Virginia Creeper	4-10
Passiflora sp.	Passionflower	9-10
Rhoicissus capensis	Cape Grape	10
Vitis sp.	Grape	6-10

Vines with Holdfasts

These vines attach to rough surfaces, such as brick or stucco buildings, wood fences, or tree trunks, with small bunches of rootlets at leaf and branch unions or flat suction cups at the ends of aerial rootlets or tendrils.

		Zones
Campsis sp.	Trumpet Creeper	4-8
Euonymus fortunei	Wintercreeper	4-8
Ficus pumila	Creeping Fig	9-10
Hedera helix	English Ivy	5-10
Hydrangea anomala	Climbing Hydrangea	5-9
Parthenocissus sp.	Boston Ivy, Virginia Creeper	4-10

Cape honeysuckle *(Tecomaria sp.)*

Wisteria *(Wisteria sp.)*

Kiwi *(Actinidia chinensis)*

Evergreen

Evergreen vines are a welcome sight in regions where cold temperatures leave many plants bare. They give year-round shade for sunny, warm climates and keep the landscape a bright, inviting green. Use these vines for permanent screens, ground covers, or arbors. A few of them will be semievergreen in the coldest limits of their growing range.

		Zones
Antigonon leptopus	Coral Vine	8-10
Beaumontia grandiflora	Herald's-Trumpet	10
Bougainvillea sp.	Bougainvillea	9-10
Clematis armandii	Evergreen Clematis	8-10
Clytostoma callistegioides	Violet Trumpet Vine	9-10
Distictis sp.	Trumpet Vine	9-10
Euonymus fortunei	Wintercreeper	4-8
x Fatshedera lizei	Fatshedera	9-10
Ficus pumila	Creeping Fig	9-10
Gelsemium sempervirens	Carolina Yellow Jessamine	7-10
Hedera helix	English Ivy	5-10
Hibbertia scandens	Gold Guinea Plant	10
Jasminum sp.	Jasmine	8-10
Passiflora sp.	Passionflower	9-10
Rhoicissus capensis	Cape Grape	10
Rosa banksiae	Banks' Rose	5-10
Tecomaria capensis	Cape Honeysuckle	9-10
Trachelospermum sp.	Star Jasmine	7-10

Deciduous

Vines that drop their leaves during winter have a valuable place in the landscape and they are among the coldhardiest of vines. They may leave the growing season in a blaze of color as does Boston ivy, revealing patterns of branches and hidden fruits; or they may enter spring festooned with flowers as does wisteria. Deciduous vines are useful in sites that need both summer shade and winter sun.

		Zones
Actinidia chinensis	Kiwi	8-10
Campsis sp.	Trumpet Creeper	4-8
Celastrus sp.	Bittersweet	3-9
Clematis sp.	Clematis	4-10
Hydrangea anomala	Climbing Hydrangea	5-9
Parthenocissus sp.	Boston Ivy, Virginia Creeper	4-10
Passiflora sp.	Passionflower	9-10
Polygonum aubertii	Silver Lace Vine	5-10
Rosa hybrids	Climbing Rose	5-10
Vitis sp.	Grape	6-10
Wisteria sp.	Wisteria	5-9

Wet Soils

These are vines that tolerate constantly moist soil that has reasonable drainage. A few, such as English ivy, are tolerant of drier soils but perform well in the wet conditions often characteristic of heavy soils with poor drainage. From this list you can choose vines to solve the problem of greenery for shady, wet places.

		Zones
Actinidia chinensis	Kiwi	8-10
Beaumontia grandiflora	Herald's-Trumpet	10
Campsis radicans	Trumpet Creeper	4-8
Clematis sp.	Clematis	4-10
x Fatshedera lizei	Fatshedera	9-10
Ficus pumila	Creeping Fig	9-10
Hedera helix	English Ivy	5-10
Hibbertia scandens	Gold Guinea Plant	10
Hydrangea anomala	Climbing Hydrangea	5-9
Jasminum sp.	Jasmine	8-10
Lonicera sp.	Honeysuckle	4-10
Parthenocissus sp.	Boston Ivy, Virginia Creeper	4-10
Passiflora sp.	Passionflower	9-10
Trachelospermum sp.	Star Jasmine	7-10
Vitis sp.	Grape	6-10
Wisteria sp.	Wisteria	5-9

Bougainvillea *(Bougainvillea sp.)*

Honeysuckle *(Lonicera sp.)*

Honeysuckle *(Lonicera sp.)*

For Containers or Houseplants

Growing vines in containers offers a wider range of options for using vines in the landscape and around the home. Place hanging or tub containers on patios or decking for greenery and color. Frost-tender vines like bougainvillea can be enjoyed during the summer and moved under cover when low temperatures threaten the plant. Many of these vines are popular in greenhouses, in window boxes, and as houseplants.

		Zones
Bougainvillea sp.	Bougainvillea	9-10
Clematis sp.	Clematis	4-10
Euonymus fortunei 'Minima'	Wintercreeper	4-8
x Fatshedera lizei	Fatshedera	9-10
Ficus pumila	Creeping Fig	9-10
Gelsemium sempervirens	Carolina Yellow Jessamine	7-10
Hedera helix	English Ivy	5-10
Hibbertia scandens	Gold Guinea Plant	10
Jasminum sp.	Jasmine	8-10
Passiflora sp.	Passionflower	9-10
Rhoicissus capensis	Cape Grape	10
Rosa hybrids	Climbing Rose	5-10
Trachelospermum sp.	Star Jasmine	7-10
Wisteria sp.	Wisteria	5-9

To Cover an Arbor or Shade a Patio

Using vines overhead for shade is a smart, attractive way to cool a sunny exposure. Dense vines can provide deep shade, while more open vines create a pleasing, dappled light. Choose a deciduous vine to let in the winter sun and screen the summer heat. A vine-covered arbor can also be used as a regal entryway, an invitation to the garden, or an accent for a special place.

		Zones
Actinidia chinensis	Kiwi	8-10
Antigonon leptopus	Coral Vine	8-10
Beaumontia grandiflora	Herald's-Trumpet	10
Bougainvillea sp.	Bougainvillea	9-10
Celastrus sp.	Bittersweet	3-9
Clematis sp.	Clematis	4-10
Distictis sp.	Trumpet Vine	9-10
Gelsemium sempervirens	Carolina Yellow Jessamine	7-10
Hedera helix	English Ivy	5-10
Hibbertia scandens	Gold Guinea Plant	10
Jasminum sp.	Jasmine	8-10
Lonicera sp.	Honeysuckle	4-10
Parthenocissus sp.	Boston Ivy, Virginia Creeper	4-10
Passiflora sp.	Passionflower	9-10
Polygonum aubertii	Silver Lace Vine	5-10
Rhoicissus capensis	Cape Grape	10
Rosa hybrids	Climbing Rose	5-10
Trachelospermum sp.	Star Jasmine	7-10
Vitis sp.	Grape	6-10
Wisteria sp.	Wisteria	5-9

Hot Climates

Hot climates put stress on leaves and roots but with the right exposure and watering schedule, these vines will thrive. Those marked with an * are drought-tolerant.

		Zones
Actinidia chinensis	Kiwi	8-10
*Antigonon leptopus**	Coral Vine	8-10
Beaumontia grandiflora	Herald's-Trumpet	10
*Bougainvillea sp.**	Bougainvillea	9-10
*Campsis sp.**	Trumpet Creeper	4-8
*Clematis sp.**	Clematis	4-10
Clytostoma callistegioides	Violet Trumpet Vine	9-10
Distictis sp.	Trumpet Vine	9-10
x Fatshedera lizei	Fatshedera	9-10
*Ficus pumila**	Creeping Fig	9-10
*Gelsemium sempervirens**	Carolina Yellow Jessamine	7-10
*Hedera helix**	English Ivy	5-10
Hibbertia scandens	Gold Guinea Plant	10
Hydrangea anomala	Climbing Hydrangea	5-9
Jasminum sp.	Jasmine	8-10
*Lonicera sp.**	Honeysuckle	4-10
*Parthenocissus sp.**	Boston Ivy, Virginia Creeper	4-10
Passiflora sp.	Passionflower	9-10
*Polygonum aubertii**	Silver Lace Vine	5-10
Rosa hybrids*	Climbing Rose	5-10
*Tecomaria capensis**	Cape Honeysuckle	9-10
Trachelospermum sp.	Star Jasmine	7-10
*Vitis sp.**	Grape	6-10
Wisteria sp.	Wisteria	5-9

65

A Guide to Top-Rated Vines

Vines are among the most versatile plants in the garden. There are varieties that can be used as ground covers, espaliers, for shade, and even as screens and hedges. They can often be planted in small spaces where almost nothing else has room to grow.

The vines described in this section were chosen because of their proven reliability and excellent performance over many years. Gardeners, growers, and horticulturists selected the vines presented here and judged them to be top-rated, based on their knowledge and actual experience.

Encyclopedia entries: Plant descriptions are alphabetized by botanical name, with the most widely used common names shown in large, dark type below the genus name. Individual entries for the top-rated vines in the genus follow. Each listing shows the climate zone the vine is adapted to, whether the plant is evergreen or deciduous, and if it bears flowers. The growth habit of the vine, size and color of flowers, plus other characteristics such as leaf size and texture, bark, fruits, and berries are described. Any cultivars or hybrids judged top-rated are discussed. Soil requirements, best planting sites, follow-up care information, and facts about any insect pests that might be problems are included.

Ideas for your landscape: Plant entries discuss ways the vine can be used in your landscape, and the accompanying photographs illustrate the beauty and utility of vines. This combination of suggestions and photography should give you lots of ideas about using vines to beautify your home and garden.

American bittersweet *(Celastrus scandens)* grows quickly, requires little care. Has bright scarlet-and-yellow berries and colorful foliage in fall.

Star jasmine *(Trachelospermum sp.)*

'Rainbow' bougainvillea *(Bougainvillea)*

Passionflower *(Passiflora sp.)*

Trumpet vine *(Clytostoma sp.)*

Kiwi *(Actinidia chinensis)* has large green leaves; bears fragrant spring flowers and edible fruit (shown below).

Coral vine *(Antigonon leptopus)* blooms from midsummer to fall; thrives in hot climates of the South and West.

Actinidia chinensis

Kiwi, Chinese Gooseberry, Yang-Tao

Zones: 8-10.
Deciduous. Flowering.

Kiwi, with its handsome large green leaves and fragrant flowers, has long been admired as an ornamental plant. It has also gained appreciation in the United States as a valuable fruiting vine for home and orchard use. The common names Chinese gooseberry and yang-tao hint of its east Asian origin. New Zealanders, the first to grow the plant commercially, called it kiwifruit. By any name, this deciduous vine is considered the most beautiful species of the genus *Actinidia.* It is well suited for covering fences, as an espalier against a wall, or for shading a patio.

When young stems and leaves first appear they are covered in bright red hairs. Leaves expand into 8-inch rounded hearts with woolly white hairs blanketing their undersides. Creamy flowers, 1-1/2 inches long, open in May, aging to a buff-yellow color. Female plants produce egg-shaped fruits that hang like ornaments from the vine. Brown and fuzzy on the outside, the flesh inside is succulent, lime-green, and dotted with edible black seeds. Kiwi fruits have a unique flavor all their own, described as tasting like a combination of banana, melon, strawberry, and gooseberry.

Kiwi is a vine for the West Coast and areas with similar climates. Mild spring and fall temperatures with hot summers are ideal. Vines are cold hardy when completely dormant but are subject to frost damage in fall and spring. To flower and set fruit, most varieties of kiwi must have between 600 and 800 hours of winter temperatures below 45°F.

Kiwi requires a well-drained soil but is not particular about soil type. However an iron deficiency may develop in alkaline soils. Provide plenty of water during the growing season to keep leaves lush. Feed with a nitrogen fertilizer before leaves emerge and after fruit sets.

Kiwi has vigorous branches that twine up to 30 feet and need a sturdy support. Pruning can either be for fruit production or to train as an ornamental vine. Flowers and fruit are produced on 1-year-old wood. Pruning cuts should be made to preserve flower buds, easily recognized by their large bulbous shape. In general, remove up to one-third of the previous year's growth for best fruiting. For an ornamental form, cut branches when they are bare, to thin and control shape.

Both male and female plants are required if fruit set is desired. Plants are labeled accordingly in the nursery. Several female varieties are available: 'Hayward' and 'Chico' are vigorous vines producing large oval fruit; 'Vincent' is similar but with a lower chilling requirement; 'Monty', 'Bruno', and 'Abbott' bear heavy crops of smaller, oblong fruit.

Antigonon leptopus

Coral Vine, Queen's-Wreath

Zones: 8-10.
Deciduous. Flowering.

This vine is ideal for hot desert and warm, humid climates of the southern states, the Southwest, and California. Native to Mexico, the beautiful coral vine, also known as corallita, mountain rose, and rosa de Montaña, thrives in summer heat and poor soils. Grows rapidly from winter-dormant tubers to reach 20 to 40 feet by summer's end.

The branches are open, airy, and cascading. Deep rose, pink, or occasionally white flowers held in long trailing sprays cover the branches in midsummer and fall. Branches often fold and curl back on themselves to clothe the vine with garlands of blooms. Flowers cut for indoor use are long-lasting. If temperatures remain warm, blossoms will hold on the vine well into fall.

Leaves have a distinctive shape like a folded heart. They make an attractive backdrop with their bright, golden-green color and can take the hottest exposures and direct sun.

Coral vine clings by tendrils at the ends of flowering branches. Until these form, the vine will need to be tied to a support to encourage upright growth. The long, flowering sprays create a lovely effect hanging from an arbor or shading a patio. Coral vine can be trained to drape from the tops of eaves and garden walls. Use it on a fence or to screen a view and to provide a long-blooming accent in the landscape. Scrambling, slender branches will quickly cover bare soil in areas where a tough ground cover is needed.

Coral vine is a maintenance-free plant needing less attention than most vines. It performs best in soils that are not too rich, producing more flowers and fewer leaves and stems. Fertilizer is not needed. Few insects or diseases bother this vine. Keep coral vine green throughout summer with regular deep watering. It is drought-tolerant but may behave as a perennial, dying back to the ground in midsummer, without water. Its thick, tuberous roots are winter hardy, sending up vigorous stems when temperatures rise in early spring. Inland frosts may cause tops to die back but the vine will renew growth quickly on remaining branches.

Prune in fall to thin branches and control growth. Coral vine may also be cut back to its base. Protect roots with mulch in Zone 8 where temperatures drop below 25°F.

Beaumontia grandiflora

Herald's-Trumpet, Easter-Lily Vine

Zone: 10.

Evergreen. Flowering.

This vine from the Himalayan Mountains is a spectacular sight from spring to summer when it is festooned with lilylike blossoms. Growth is lush and strong with woody stems twining and arching to form a vine of grand proportions. It will reach 15 to 30 feet.

Herald's-trumpet *(Beaumontia grandiflora)* is an evergreen vine of grand proportions. Blossoms, shown below, are sweetly scented.

Bougainvillea *(Bougainvillea sp.)* is a robust grower used widely in temperate landscapes. Spectacular when in full bloom. Cultivars with variegated foliage, as shown below, are available.

Leaves are 6 to 9 inches, and have a bright, clean, glossy surface that adds a bold and tropical look to the landscape. Sweetly scented blossoms are white, tipped with pink, and have green veins on the throats. These funnel-shaped, 5-inch flowers are held in copious clusters at branch ends. Long, cylindrical pods follow in autumn.

Herald's-trumpet makes a beautiful accent plant for large gardens. Use it to cover a fence or patio, espalier against a sunny wall, or train up a column for camouflage. With diligent pruning and plenty of growing room, herald's-trumpet forms a mounding shrub. Substantial woody branches can hold the vine as a small tree, if trained and supported at an early age.

Herald's-trumpet has tuberous roots that need an unconstrained rooting zone. Plant in rich, composted soil that is deep and well-drained. For lush growth, give ample water and fertilizer in early spring before flowering. Plant in full sun.

Herald's-trumpet is a broadly growing vine that needs room to spread. Train the vine early and provide sturdy support for its heavy branches. Thin branches to reduce the mass of older vines. Flowers are produced on old wood. When pruning, in fall, retain some 1- to 3-year-old wood for good flower production the following year.

Herald's-trumpet is relatively pest-free.

Bougainvillea

Bougainvillea

Zones: 9-10.
Evergreen to partially deciduous.
Flowering.

Of all the flowering vines in the California landscape, bougainvillea, with its spectacular flowers, is the most eye-catching. The colorful part of the bougainvillea flower is made up of 3 showy bracts that surround small white flowers. These bracts carpet the vine with vibrant color, in a spectrum from magenta, purple-pink, and crimson, to shades of bronze, orange, yellow, and white. In warm areas blooming is so prolific that color can last nearly year-round. When the vine is out of flower, the soft green, heart-shaped leaves create a dense foliage.

Bougainvillea has a wide range of garden uses, from ground covers to patio covers. Besides adding brilliant splashes of color in the landscape, they are used to shade, to beautify fences and walls, and to scramble over sunny slopes. Bougainvillea is a robust grower. If given something to twine around, strong branches can quickly cover the sides of houses. Vigor and shape will vary within the different cultivars. A few, such as 'Temple Fire', are shrubby vines for use as ground covers or container plants. Anticipate rapid growth with most vining types and allow plenty of room for spreading, unless pruned frequently.

Bougainvillea is a tropical, frost-sensitive vine suitable for the hottest exposures. You can extend its growing range to Zones 8 and cold parts of Zone 9 by protecting young plants for a year or two until firmly established. In Zone 8, plant against sun-exposed walls to benefit from reflected heat. Container-grown plants can be moved to a sheltered spot when frost is expected. Established plants will quickly recover from moderate frost damage. Ripen the wood against frost by reducing water late in the growing season.

Dry gardens in the West are the ideal setting for this vine. Water the plant to get it established and bring on new growth, then minimize watering for increased flowering. Bougainvilleas grow best in soils that are well drained but not too rich. A balanced fertilizer may be added in early spring but is usually not necessary. Give roots plenty of space in an area where they will be warmed by sun or reflected heat.

Care should be taken when first setting out new plants as bougainvillea suffers a severe setback if its rootball is disturbed during planting. Gently cut bougainvillea containers in 3 or 4 locations and carefully peel the sides away. Or plant leaving it in the metal container, which will eventually disintegrate. Put them in the ground during the spring to extend the growing time so the vine is well established before cold weather.

It takes a sturdy structure to hold bougainvillea's woody branches. Vines need to be tied to their support, otherwise, branches whip in the wind, shredding the soft leaves. Withstands heavy pruning. If cut to the base in spring or fall, the plant will return to bloom the next season. Throughout the growing season, sucker growth and long branches should be removed to shape the plant and reduce its volume. A shrub form may be achieved by regular clipping throughout the year.

Bougainvillea may be bothered by the following pests: aphids, mealybugs, caterpillars, and scale. Control them at the first signs of damage with an appropriate pesticide.

Two species of bougainvillea contribute to the wide array of flower colors and growth habits. The lesser bougainvillea, *B. glabra,* has long-lasting flowers with less vigorous growth. *Bougainvillea spectabilis* or the Brazilian bougainvillea is the more showy of the two and can tolerate cooler temperatures.

Campsis

Trumpet Creeper

Trumpet creepers are aggressive deciduous vines that bear spectacular flowers. They are suitable for large spaces.

Leaves are compound, having 7 to 11 leaflets with serrated margins. The vine is in peak form in midsummer when the showy blossoms appear. Terminal clusters hold 6 to 12 brilliant, 3-inch flowers shaped like funnels with wide, open mouths. Flowers, colored orange to scarlet, attract hummingbirds.

Trumpet creepers can grow up to 30 feet, with aerial rootlets attaching stems to rough surfaces. Grow these vines over large stone walls, as a filler against fences in expansive

Bougainvillea *(Bougainvillea sp.)* can reach massive proportions in the hot, dry climates of the West.

Bougainvillea 'Rainbow' below left; *Bougainvillea* 'Jamaica White' below right.

Madame Galen trumpet creeper *(Campsis x tagliabuana* 'Madame Galen') is vigorous and cold hardy. Flower clusters, shown below, are colorful and dramatic.

gardens, or up the trunks of tall trees. Roots send out suckers, spreading vines over large areas. These suckers should be removed if the vines threaten to become too invasive. Trumpet creepers can be pruned into a large hedge if trained at an early age.

Trumpet creeper rootlets are not tenacious clingers. Young vines need support until clinging rootlets form. High winds can separate top-heavy branches from their support. This can be avoided by pruning to reduce the volume of branches, and by pinching growing tips to encourage growth at the base of branches. Remove deadwood and excessive growth, retaining the flower-bearing young branches.

Grow trumpet creepers in full sun. Plants are most attractive if given a rich soil and average water but can withstand less desirable conditions.

Campsis grandiflora
Chinese Trumpet Creeper
Zones: 7-8.
Deciduous. Flowering.

Chinese trumpet creeper has large scarlet blossoms in midsummer. Leaflets grow 7 to 9 on a stem. A good choice for smaller gardens because its growth is restrained.

Campsis radicans
Trumpet Creeper Vine
Zones: 4-8.
Deciduous. Flowering.

This native American vine grows vigorously to 40 feet. Leaves have 9 to 11 leaflets on a stem. Orange blossoms marked with red appear in mid-July. They are 3 inches long, with expanded lips. Five-inch-long capsules hang through winter. The vine dies to the ground where temperatures are freezing but tops regrow in spring. 'Flava' has yellow flowers.

Campsis x tagliabuana
'Madame Galen'
Madame Galen Trumpet Creeper
Zones: 4-8.
Deciduous. Flowering.

This is the top-rated hybrid of the two *Campsis* species. Salmon-red flowers are held in loose clusters. Reaches 25 to 30 feet high and has the cold hardiness of the trumpet creeper.

Celastrus
Bittersweet

Both American and Oriental bittersweet are woody, twining deciduous vines best used in naturalistic landscapes. They are in their glory in fall, when leaves drop to expose scarlet-and-yellow berries that last through the season.

Bittersweet is a fast, vigorous grower, requiring little care. Avoid planting near small trees and shrubs because the twining vines will use them as supports, eventually smothering the plants with strong encircling stems. With careful pruning, vines make effective covers for an arbor, fence, or sturdy trellis. When used as a ground cover, branches circle around themselves forming a dense, mounded mat that is good over rocky banks and in open spaces.

Leaves are roundish and light green, changing to bright yellow before dropping in fall. Greenish-white flowers appear in late spring but are small and inconspicuous. Green fruits change to yellow-orange in fall, then burst open, revealing masses of beautiful scarlet berries. Before heavy frost, cut the ornamental branches for a lasting indoor decoration. Flowers occur on separate plants and both sexes are required for berry production. Plant male and female vines close together for best fruit set.

Bittersweet is an adaptable vine. Few vines can match its tolerance of cold winter temperatures and high winds found in the midwestern and northeastern states. It is less common in warm winter regions because fruiting is best with winter chill. Boggy, wet soils are not suitable. Bittersweet is drought-tolerant and grows well in poor, sandy soil.

Prune severely every year in early spring, before leaves appear. Flowers and fruit are produced on new wood. A harsh pruning will help contain twining stems and prevent tangling.

Scale may be a problem on bittersweet. Watch for signs of infestation and treat with an appropriate control.

Celastrus orbiculatus
Oriental Bittersweet
Zones: 5-9.
Deciduous. Flowering.

Oriental bittersweet is a vigorous grower, spreading up to 40 feet. It is used to cover large areas. Very round leaves and lateral fruiting branches characterize this species.

Celastrus scandens
American Bittersweet
Zones: 3-9.
Deciduous. Flowering.

American bittersweet is a rapidly spreading vine with oval, light green, 4-inch leaves. It can be distinguished from Oriental bittersweet by the way its fruit is held in terminal clusters above the leaves. The plant is more contained than the Asian species, reaching 10 to 20 feet at maturity. This vine can be seen growing wild in its native range of eastern North America.

Clematis

Clematis

Clematis are considered the "Queen of Climbers" because of their beautiful flowers and fine form. Both deciduous and evergreen species are available. A wide variety of colors and flower sizes has been developed, resulting in over 100 named cultivars. Flowers have many shapes, varying from large open saucers to dainty bells. Many shades of pink, purple, mauve, blue, lavender, and white blossoms are available. Long-lasting as cut flowers; the feathery seed pods also are beautiful in arrangements.

Clematis forms slender, twisting stems that make well-mannered vines for use in large or small landscapes. Plant where flowers can be admired—beside a lamppost or a

The scarlet berries of American bittersweet *(Celastrus scandens)* stand out against the yellow fall foliage color and look dramatic after the leaves drop.

Evergreen clematis *(Clematis armandii* 'Apple Blossom') blooms in early spring.

Clematis *(Clematis sp.)*

Evergreen clematis *(Clematis armandii)* bears fragrant white flowers in early spring. Has twining, cascading branches.

porch railing, or against a prominent wall or fence. If left to scramble, clematis forms a beautiful ground cover on banks. Indoor gardeners can successfully grow clematis in pots in sunny windows.

If a few simple rules for growing clematis are followed, you will be rewarded with healthy, vibrant plants. First, choose a variety suited to your climate zone with the form of flower you prefer. Then, plant the vine properly by preparing a deep planting hole that has been amended with ample organic matter for maximum aeration. Clematis grows best in neutral to slightly alkaline soils. Add lime to acid soil or bone meal to alkaline soil to meet this requirement. Locate the vines where the foliage will be in full sun or light shade but where the roots will be cool and shaded. Such a location is needed to promote blooming. Stem rot occurs when clematis is planted too shallowly. Place the crown of the plant 2 to 3 inches deep and cover with soil. A layer of mulch will help keep roots cool and discourage weeds. Clematis are shallow-rooted vines and will not disturb nearby plants.

Once the vine is set in place, young stems should be tied to supports. A light trellis is adequate to support twining stems. Stems of clematis are fragile and break easily. Tie them carefully.

Apply balanced fertilizer once a year during the growing season. Clematis thrive in a moist, well-drained soil, and need watering regularly.

There are two strategies for pruning clematis. Both encourage flowering but differ in timing. The varieties that bloom in early summer to fall should have current season wood pruned after flowering, either in early fall or the following spring when the buds swell. Plants pruned back to within 6 to 12 inches from the ground will grow bushy and produce maximum new wood.

Midspring-flowering clematis produce buds on the previous year's wood. They should be pruned lightly by thinning branches and removing seedheads after flowering.

The following descriptions indicate the diversity of clematis' flower and plant form.

Clematis armandii
Evergreen Clematis, Armand Clematis
Zones: 8-10.
Evergreen. Flowering.

Shiny, dark green foliage throughout the year makes this clematis a good background or accent plant. Leaves are 4 to 6 inches long, leathery and narrow, with 3 prominent veins. They are held in 3's on slender drooping stems. White fragrant blossoms, 1 to 2-1/2 inches wide, grace the vine in early spring. Long, plump seed pods follow in summer.

A beautiful vine to drape along the tops of eaves and fences, or to use as a lavish cover on a strong arbor. Bare tree trunks serve as an excellent support for this clematis, adding greenery where it may be needed.

Evergreen clematis tolerates heat if given partial shade. Grow the vine in full sun in coastal locations. Supply ample water in arid climates and mulch the soil to keep the roots cool and moist. Prune soon after blooming because flowers are borne on old wood.

'Apple Blossom' is a light pink variety suitable for warm regions.

Clematis x jackmanii
Jackman Clematis
Zones: 5-10.
Evergreen or deciduous.
Flowering.

Jackman clematis was the first large-flowered hybrid developed, and continues to be an all-time favorite. It is admired for its abundant, velvety, deep purple flowers that open flat and are 4 to 6 inches wide. They appear from July to October.

Jackman clematis has a delicate appearance with neat foliage and slender stems. Twisting stems need guidance over a supporting framework to prevent tangling. Its 12- to 15-foot growth can reach to the top of high fences. Arbors and trellis-work are good supports.

A deep, well-drained soil is essential to Jackman clematis' getting established. Keep roots moist and shaded. Flowers are produced on new wood. Branches should be cut in early spring just before new growth begins to within 2 feet, or 2 or 3 buds from the ground. Vines die to the ground in cold areas but regrow in spring.

Several varieties have come from this strain. 'Comtess de Bouchaud' is a silvery-pink-flowered form; 'Mme Edouard Andre' has purple-red blossoms; 'Perle d' Azur' is pale blue.

Clematis texensis
Scarlet Clematis
Zones: 4-10.
Deciduous. Flowering.

The showiest of our native clematis, scarlet clematis produces 1-inch, scarlet, bell-shaped flowers copiously from July to the first frost. Beautiful seed pods then become silvery plumes covering the plant. Glossy, thick leaves with 4 to 8 leaflets are an attractive feature. Scarlet clematis is a rapid-growing, compact vine that forms a lush mass suitable for low fences.

Scarlet clematis can tolerate dry periods but prefers a moist, well-drained soil. Protect the vine from strong winds. Flowers are produced on new wood, and plants should be pruned in early spring, before new growth begins.

These varieties offer a choice of flower color: 'Comtess de Onslow' with scarlet-banded violet-purple blossoms; 'Duchess of Albany' with pink flowers and brown centers; 'Etoile Rose' bears cerise-pink blooms with silver margins.

Clytostoma callistegioides

Violet Trumpet Vine

Zones: 9-10.
Evergreen. Flowering.

This tropical vine is a robust plant, growing to 40 feet high with a 15-to-20-foot spread. Long drooping branches hang gracefully from the vine and drape comfortably over tall fences or the eaves of buildings.

Clematis *(Clematis sp.)* grow best with their branches in full sun and their roots shaded and mulched.

Violet trumpet vine *(Clytostoma callistegioides)*

Violet trumpet vine *(Clytostoma callistegioides)* is a robust grower of graceful habit. Covers a sturdy fence in regal splendor. Flowers shown below.

When festooned with orchid-colored blossoms from midspring to fall it creates a lovely, soft effect in the garden. Delicate 3-inch flowers are held in terminal clusters. They are an open trumpet shape, colored violet, and streaked with deep purple to their throats. Evergreen leaves are divided in pairs and are glossy, deep green with wavy leaf margins. Violet trumpet vine clings by tendrils to a wall or fence, but tendrils are not strong and the vines require securing to most surfaces.

On a large fence this vine becomes a colorful screen and a lasting green cover. It is also excellent when used to create a lush tropical effect near a pool or patio. Use on a tall embankment, or to cascade over a rock wall.

Violet trumpet vine grows well and remains evergreen in the coastal and warm inland areas of California, Florida and parts of the Gulf States. It can be grown in Zone 8. The roots will survive a low of 10°F if covered with a protective layer of mulch.

Adaptable to both sun and shade, this vine tolerates windy locations and is relatively pest-free. Nearly any garden soil, from clay to sandy texture, is acceptable. For best results provide good drainage and regular watering. Apply a balanced fertilizer in early spring.

Violet trumpet vine will need a strong support for its heavy mass of branches. Begin training the vine when young to direct growth. Stems should be tied to the support if grown in an upright form. Pruning during late winter will help remove tangling branches, reduce branch volume, and direct growth. Pruning also encourages flowering. Cut back long branches and spent blossoms throughout the growing season to keep the plant attractive.

Distictis

Trumpet Vine

Glorious, trumpet-shaped flowers for several months are ample reward for anyone who grows either of these two top-rated vines. Native to Mexico, they give a tropical look to warm weather gardens of the Gulf States and California. Trumpet vines belong to a large group of flowering plants in the Bignonia family. Formerly classified either in the genus *Phaedranthus* or *Bignonia,* they have now been given the botanical name *Distictis.*

Robust growers, climbing 20 to 30 feet by clinging tendrils, trumpet vines make excellent screens, arbors, or flowering wall covers. Grow in full sun near the coast or in a protected, shady location inland. Both vines are easy to grow and relatively pest-free. They thrive in most soils with good drainage if watered regularly. The evergreen foliage can be damaged by temperatures below 24°F. Give vines protection in colder, inland areas.

Distictis buccinatoria

Blood-Red Trumpet Vine

Zones: 9-10.

Evergreen. Flowering.

This trumpet vine is spectacular when its long, yellow-throated, crimson flowers are in bloom. Blossoms, which are held out from the foliage, fade to rose-red before dropping, and will color the garden from May to early fall. Where the weather remains warm they often bloom almost continuously. Heavy masses of lustrous green leaves make an attractive display year-round. Oval 2-inch leaves are held on twining branches ending with a 3-parted clinging tendril. When grown on a fence or arbor, provide strong support for the vigorous branches. Prune heavily after blossoms drop to control the plant's shape and size. Left unpruned, plants grow billowy and top-heavy.

Blood-red trumpet vine prefers a well-drained, loamy soil but is tolerant of most garden soils. Fertilize and water regularly to encourage young plants. A robust grower once established.

Of the two top-rated trumpet vines, this species is the best choice for inland areas. It tolerates more intense heat and colder temperatures.

Distictis laxiflora
Vanilla Trumpet Vine
Zones: 9-10.
Evergreen. Flowering.

Several months of the year, this enchanting vine fills the air with the delicious fragrance of vanilla. The 3-inch-long trumpet flowers open purple, fading to orchid and white before dropping. They are held in terminal clusters on slender stems during warm months. In some areas they bloom for up to 8 months. Dark green leaves are oblong in shape and the last tendril of the growing shoot is unbranched, distinguishing it from the 3-parted tendril of blood-red trumpet vine.

Vanilla trumpet vine is a superb grower but never becomes rampant. Requires only light pruning to maintain its neat appearance. Use as a light screen for fences, against a wall, or on an arbor or pergola. Makes a wonderful patio plant, where its prolonged bloom and fragrant flowers can be enjoyed up close.

Vanilla trumpet vine requires average garden conditions. Provide a moderately well-drained soil and even moisture. Thrives in the warm coastal belt of California. Takes some sun but prefers partial shade. Protect from wind.

Blood-red trumpet vine *(Distictis buccinatoria)* provides year-round greenery; blooms from midspring to fall. Flowers shown below.

Euonymus fortunei
Wintercreeper, Evergreen Bittersweet
Zones: 4-8.
Evergreen.

This attractive plant is often used as a substitute for ivy *(Hedera sp.)* because of its extremely adaptable nature. It is useful from the cold areas in the Midwest and Northeast to the hot desert areas of the Southwest.

Wintercreeper is a trailing vine or low-growing shrub with rootlike

Purple-leaf euonymus *(Euonymus fortunei* 'Colorata') is bright green in summer (as shown below) and changes to purple in fall, adding welcome color to the winter landscape.

holdfasts. It is one of the most popular evergreen vines for covering walls, fences, and bare ground.

The fine-textured foliage is handsome, and the stems spread evenly. A typical leaf has a rounded oval shape 1 or 2 inches across, with scalloped margins. Leaves form a neat, glossy green carpet over the branches.

As with English ivy, the leaves and branches can take two forms. The juvenile form is more often planted. Slender clinging stems bear small leaves and do not flower or fruit. Occasionally, a juvenile plant will send out branches of mature growth, which can be removed by pruning. In the mature form, stronger bushy branches extend out from the plant and produce inconspicuous flowers and colorful scarlet fruit. Leaves are larger and more leathery in texture. Plants propagated from mature wood have an upright shrublike shape.

The restrained growth of wintercreeper makes it a good plant for the low-maintenance garden. Only occasional spring pruning is needed to direct growth against a wall or keep it within bounds. Vines need no support to climb on brick, concrete, or shingle walls.

Easy culture is one of wintercreeper's greatest virtues. Roots are not particular about soil type, growing well in clay or sandy soils. Grows in sun to partial shade. In the coldest regions leaves may sunburn during the winter. In these areas the vine should be planted where it has some protection.

A well-drained, moist soil is ideal for encouraging rooting along stems to form a dense ground cover. Space plants 1 to 2 feet apart. Stems will root as they trail, making it a good plant for erosion control on slopes. Mulch soil to discourage weeds. Once established, wintercreeper's dense mat will shade out all but the most tenacious weeds.

As with its relative bittersweet, wintercreeper is subject to infestations of euonymus scale. This sometimes severe pest appears as whitish dots on stems and the undersides of leaves. Control with dormant oil sprays and by removing heavily infested branches.

Wintercreeper was once classified as *Euonymus radicans* but is now called *Euonymus fortunei.* It may be sold under both names. The following varieties have unique characteristics and are top-rated for landscape use.

'Colorata', purple-leaf euonymus, is used for its fall and winter color. Leaves change from green to a lovely reddish purple. Growth is more restrained than the species. Responds well to shaping. Good used on a low wall or as a ground cover. The cultivar 'Gracilis' has leaves variegated with creamy-white that turn pink in cold weather. A slow-growing trailer suitable for small areas and containers. 'Minima', baby wintercreeper, makes a fine-textured wall or ground cover, with tiny, 1/2-inch leaves. 'Kewensis' is similar to 'Minima' with even smaller leaves and more contained growth. 'Silver Queen' is a slow-growing vine with white leaf margins. Does not cling tenaciously. 'Vegeta', big-leaf wintercreeper, is a mounding, shrubby form with orange fruit in fall. Grows 4 feet high and spreads to cover an area 15 to 20 feet square. Good used against walls.

x Fatshedera lizei

Fatshedera, Botanical-Wonder

Zones: 9-10.
Evergreen. Flowering.

Fatshedera is known as a botanical-wonder because of its unusual origin. In 1911, Lize Freres raised this plant by crossing plants from 2 different genera—*Fatsia japonica,* Japanese aralia, and *Hedera helix,* English ivy. Their names were combined to make *Fatshedera.*

The characteristics of both parents are reflected in the hybrid's growth and habit. It forms a semi-erect shrub, sending out long, rope-like branches bearing large, shiny, evergreen leaves. Long trailing stems need to be supported if they are to climb. If the growing tips are pinched back, the plant takes on a shrubby look similar to aralia.

Long spikes of greenish-white flowers appear in fall but it is the luxuriant foliage that makes fatshedera such a desirable specimen plant for use both in the garden and indoors. Large-lobed leaves with pointed ends are 5 to 9 inches in length and width and are rich glossy green, adding a tropical feel to the landscape. 'Variegata' has white-bordered leaves, providing added visual interest.

Use this decorative plant in a poolside setting or shaded entryway. When trained on a fence or placed against a wall, it makes an attractive background for flowers and shrubs. Use on a trellis, for an espalier, or as a screen. Young stems are flexible and easy to train. Branches need to be tied securely, but not tightly, to their support. Planted in a tub, fatshedera is a popular houseplant or accent plant for patio use.

Fatshedera is adapted outdoors to the South, Southeast, Southwest, and California. It tolerates deep shade to full sun in cool coastal regions. Otherwise, leaves need protection from dry winds and hot sun. Young new growth is susceptible to cold temperatures and requires protection from early and late frost.

Provide a rich, well-drained soil and plenty of moisture. Periodic spring and midsummer feedings with a nitrogen fertilizer will keep leaves lush and green. Pinch growing tips to encourage branching at the base. Lower stems tend to become bare as the plant grows upward. If you want to make a new start, prune heavily, almost to the ground. Fatshedera will serve as a ground cover if laterals are kept pruned throughout the growing season and long branches are secured to the ground.

When growing fatshedera as a houseplant, place it near a window or where it will receive bright, indirect light. Do not overwater, and watch for common pests such as aphids and spider mites.

Fatshedera *(x Fatshedera lizei)* forms a bold evergreen background for colorful companion plants. Foliage shown below.

Creeping fig *(Ficus pumila)* provides dense year-round greenery; occupies minimum space. Surface-hugging foliage shown below.

Ficus pumila

Creeping Fig

Zones: 9-10.
Evergreen.

Small, thin leaves and delicate creeping stems give little indication that this vine is a relative of the expansive, fruiting fig trees common to orchard and garden. However, its vigor should not be underestimated. Creeping fig can cover broad faces of buildings or rock walls. Tiny rootlike holdfasts cling firmly to wood, glass, or stone. Branching, wiry stems form a delicate tracery over its supportive surface. Deeply veined, heart-shaped leaves are held flat against the stems and eventually form a dense mat.

As with ivy, *Hedera sp.*, the character of the new stems and leaves changes as the plant grows older. Small, 1-inch leaves on clinging stems are borne by young plants. The mature form bears large, leathery foliage on coarse branches that hang away from the tight mass of juvenile foliage. Mature branches produce inedible figlike fruits. Prune out mature stems to maintain the attractive juvenile form.

Creeping fig makes an effective screen for narrow spaces where greenery is desired. It is also suitable for use in containers or hanging baskets for an entryway or patio. Indoors on a trellis or hung near a sunny window, it makes an attractive houseplant.

While getting established, creeping fig needs to be tied to a support until holdfasts develop. Pinching growing tips will encourage branching. To keep the plant within bounds, thin out and cut back the stems occasionally. This will reduce the mass and discourage adult growth from forming.

Partial shade is necessary for creeping fig to thrive and leaves to stay dark green. Vigorous roots prefer a rich, moist soil but can tolerate occasional dry periods. Misting branches encourages the growth of rooting holdfasts and lush leaves. Creeping fig performs best in warm mild climates where temperatures do not fall below 24°F. Providing protection with a wall or overhang will extend its range to the cooler zones of California, the Southwest, and the South.

Two varieties are available with differing leaf shapes. Leaves of *Ficus pumila* 'Quercifolia' are lobed and resemble tiny oak leaves. The variety 'Minima' resembles the standard form but has smaller, daintier leaves.

Gelsemium sempervirens

Carolina Yellow Jessamine

Zones: 7-10.
Evergreen. Flowering

This vine, native from Virginia to Texas, is the state flower of South Carolina. In early spring, its fragrant, bright yellow blossoms appear, filling the air with fragrance. An open, cascading vine, Carolina yellow jessamine is a welcome addition in any garden.

Carolina yellow jessamine has a moderate growth rate; the slender, reddish-brown stems climb by twisting, eventually reaching 20 feet. Long branches cascade from a wall or drape over a fence and bear glossy lance-shaped leaves 1 to 4 inches long. Funnel-shaped flowers cover the vine from spring into summer in Zones 7 and 8; nearly year-round in Zones 9 and 10. During the peak of bloom, it is blanketed with yellow flowers.

An adaptable vine, Carolina yellow jessamine can serve as an evergreen screen or patio shade, or a ground cover on banks. In containers, the plant makes a versatile potted vine. It grows indoors near a sunny window, and in hanging baskets or on a trellis it makes a colorful houseplant.

Carolina yellow jessamine tolerates both full sun and partial shade and adapts to a wide range of soil types. In a windy location, the branches swing gracefully in the breeze. It performs best with regular watering but is known to be moderately drought-tolerant for short times. It is easy to grow and pest-free.

Carolina yellow jessamine is restrained in its growth, making pruning an easy chore. Tie young stems to a sturdy support. Pruning should be done in fall once the vine matures; cut back side shoots and prune to desired shape. If the vine becomes top-heavy, cut back severely to renew growth and thin out branches. Keep the vine pruned to 3 feet if grown as a ground cover. A heavy pruning will also reduce the mass and encourage new branches. A mild fertilizer can be applied in early spring and after flowering.

Carolina yellow jessamine is reportedly a poisonous plant. No parts of it should be eaten.

Hedera

Ivy

Historically, ivy is a prominent plant. It has been glorified in legends, graced the world's most famed gardens, and inspired artists and poets for centuries.

Hedera canariensis

Algerian Ivy

Zones: 8-10.

Evergreen.

Algerian ivy, used primarily as a vining ground cover, has large, 5- to 7-inch leaves with distinctive red stems. Less drought-tolerant and cold hardy than English ivy. The variety 'Variegata' has leaves edged in white.

Hedera helix

English Ivy

Zones: 5-10.

Evergreen.

English horticulturists refer to *Hedera helix* simply as 'The Ivy' and have embraced it as their most-prized vine. Over the years nearly 100 varieties have been developed, each with it own unique leaf shape and color.

English ivy is a dependable, hardy, evergreen vine whose use in the landscape is limited only by

Carolina yellow jessamine *(Gelsemium sempervirens)* is an adaptable vine; covered with fragrant yellow blooms in spring. Flowers shown below.

English ivy *(Hedera helix)* is a hardy multipurpose evergreen vine that grows in full sun or shade. Covers ground, fences, or buildings with luxuriant greenery.

one's imagination. As an upright vine, the aerial rootlets cling to the sides of buildings, creating a blanket of greenery. The plant's rootlets are tenacious and can pull paint off wood, or chip fragments from bricks when removed. On a fence, the plant can become hedge-like, forming a thick mass of leaves. As a trailing plant it forms a neat, lush ground cover. It grows vigorously by sidewalks, or in median strips and is easily contained. Branching, rooting stems prevent hillside erosion.

For the more adventurous gardener, English ivy can be manipulated into fanciful shapes. It works well as a topiary form, espaliered into intricate wall patterns, or garlanded over windows and entryways. Indoors and out, English ivy is a handsome plant for hanging baskets and trellis-work.

Typically, English ivy leaves are 2 to 4 inches in length and width with a glossy, leathery green surface. The 5 lobes are wedge-shaped and veins are defined by their pale color. Variations on this theme have been developed by careful selection of desired characteristics. You can find ruffled edges, fans, heart shapes, bird's feet, tricolors, and every type of variegation. Varieties with interesting leaf form and variegation make striking accents.

Ivy exhibits an interesting phenomenon—leaf shape and plant habit can change unpredictably. Ivy changes from its *juvenile state*, the form most often planted, to an *arborescent* or *mature state*. In the mature state, leaves are generally squarish and unlobed on non-clinging, bushy branches. These branches produce inconspicuous flowers and fruits. The variety 'Arborescens' is a shrubby type selected from mature branches.

The change from juvenile to mature form can occur when an upright, clinging branch grows beyond its support. Pruning prevents mature branches from forming.

English ivy is relatively easy to grow. Once established, vines can be maintained with occasional pruning and pest control programs. A neutral-to-alkaline, well-drained, moist soil is the ideal growing medium. However, a wide range of soil types is tolerated. Amending the soil with organic matter will promote rooting and fast growth when ivy is used as a ground cover. Ivy makes its fastest, most lush growth if given adequate moisture. Water in the morning so the leaves will dry out by evening. This reduces the incidence of disease. When planting as a ground cover, space plants 12 to 18 inches apart. Keep the area moist to prevent wilting. Control weeds until the ivy forms its own dense cover. Apply a nitrogen fertilizer in early spring.

English ivy's tolerance of full sun or the deepest shade contributes to its usefulness in the landscape. Partial shade is needed however in the hot desert to prevent sunburn and in the coldest climates to prevent winterkill of leaves.

Ivy can withstand considerable pruning to direct its growth and control volume. Shear edges 2 to 3 times a year for a neat appearance along walkways and fences. Mowing of ground covers in early spring will reduce the mass and encourage new growth. Leaves form quickly to replace those removed.

Ivy does have some pest problems. When a potential problem is spotted, select an appropriate method to control the pest. Keep ivy pruned to discourage nesting birds and rodents.

The following are the most popular varieties of English ivy used in the landscape. They are just a few of the numerous forms that are grown.

'Aureo-variegata' has beautiful yellow-variegated foliage. 'Baltica' is one of the hardiest varieties for Zone 4; has whiter veins and smaller leaves than its parent. 'Bulgaria' is cold hardy in Zone 5 and somewhat drought-tolerant. '238th Street', discovered on this street in New York City, is one of the most cold hardy with heart-shaped leaves; not subject to sunburn. 'Digitata' is a 5- to 7-lobed variety. 'Fluffy Ruffles' has small leaves with wavy margins; good in small spaces. 'Gold Heart' has large yellow center markings on smooth leaves.

Hibbertia scandens

Gold Guinea Plant

Zone: 10.
Evergreen. Flowering.

Gold guinea vine is a luxuriant, twining plant from Australia that is well adapted to the warm, frost-free regions of the southern United States and California. It is a handsome vine with clean dense foliage year-round. Slender, reddish-brown stems carry it to 15 feet to form a tall shrubby vine. Left unsupported, the dense branches make a tidy ground cover.

Bright yellow flowers, which account for its name, adorn the plant from late spring to early fall, making it an excellent accent plant. The five-petaled blossoms look like small wild roses and are especially attractive against the glossy dark green leaves. Flowers are lightly scented, with a musky odor. Leaves have winged stem attachments and their undersides are covered with fine silky hairs.

Gold guinea plant is a rapid grower. It is an excellent choice for a partly shaded patio, an entryway, or a fence. Its neat form makes it a good choice for small spaces or container growing, but it will need pruning to restrain its growth. It also performs nicely as a ground cover if partly shaded.

Gold guinea plant will thrive if given ample water and protected from hot, reflected sun. Light frost may burn the leaves but damage is only temporary. New foliage soon restores its lush appearance. Gold guinea plant is best grown in moist, well-drained soil. If exposed to drying winds or dry soil, the plant may be vulnerable to insect infestations. Otherwise it is relatively pest-free.

Prune to reduce top growth and keep the vine within 15 to 20 feet. Remove unwanted branches. Prune in early spring before flowering or in fall after blossoms fade.

Gold guinea plant *(Hibbertia scandens)* is a fast-growing, clean-foliaged vine for frost-free climates. Flowers, shown below, are borne in summer.

Climbing hydrangea *(Hydrangea anomala)* is very hardy. Lacy white flowers stand out against the bright green leaves.

Chinese jasmine *(Jasminum polyanthum)*

Hydrangea anomala

Climbing Hydrangea

Zones: 5-9.
Deciduous. Flowering.

This vine produces dramatic blossoms and grows on a grand scale, covering tall buildings with its bold foliage and sturdy stems. It can cling to any supporting surface with its aerial rootlets and frequently climbs over 50 feet. Although its growth rate is slow at the start, climbing hydrangea becomes a dense, vigorous grower once established.

This vine is in its full glory by late spring when clusters of showy white blossoms cover the plant with lacy caps. They are prominently displayed, held away from the foliage on stems 1 to 3 feet long. Flower clusters are flat, open, and 6 to 8 inches across.

Large, bright green, lustrous leaves appear in spring. Their heart shape and fine-toothed edges make them particularly handsome. Leaves drop in fall, but reveal the shedding red bark, which adds to the vine's beauty.

This decorative vine should be used on large surfaces in scale with the size of its flowers and leaves. Place it against big expanses of masonry walls, on a tall chimney, or as a climber in a large tree. Climbing hydrangea is best supported on an indestructible surface because rootlets can damage wood structures. If unsupported, the vine becomes a rambling creeping shrub.

Climbing hydrangea is a hardy vine. It withstands the cold temperatures of Zone 5 yet tolerates the semi-arid conditions of the Southwest. It is not usually damaged in windy areas. Diseases and pests are rare.

Provide a rich, composted soil that is moist and well drained. In early spring apply a balanced formula fertilizer.

Prune climbing hydrangea to maintain its symmetry and reduce mass. Heavy pruning in winter or early spring will restrain its robust nature.

Jasminum

Jasmine

True jasmines are unmistakeable when the sweet fragrance of their blooms fills the garden air. Angel-wing, *Jasminum nitidum,* and Chinese jasmine, *Jasminum polyanthum,* are top-rated vining species. They have a graceful, neat habit with leathery green leaves. The evergreen foliage makes a fine backdrop for the plentiful and long-lasting flowers.

Jasmines are versatile landscape plants in warm climates; elsewhere grow them in a greenhouse. Support the twining stems by providing something secure for them to wrap around such as a post or a fence, or drape them over an entryway. Both species grow well as luxuriant ground covers in part shade or full sun. They grow best in moist, well-drained soil and are easy to care for and relatively pest-free. An annual pruning and occasional fertilizing are all that is required to keep jasmine vines healthy.

Jasminum nitidum

Angel-Wing Jasmine

Zone: 10.
Evergreen. Flowering.

Angel-wing jasmine blooms in late spring and summer in the southern states and California. It flowers most abundantly where temperatures remain warm throughout its long growing period. Desert climates are ideal. The vine is considered semideciduous where temperatures drop below 32°F, but roots will survive at temperatures to 25°F.

When in bloom this jasmine is covered with highly fragrant blossoms that look like pinwheels. Flowers are white above and purple on the underside, measure 1 to 1-1/2 inches long, and are held in clusters of 3 on slender stalks. Leathery-textured foliage is an attractive background for the abundant flowers. The leaves are distinguished by their somewhat glossy surface and 3-inch-long, oval shape.

Angel-wing jasmine grows at a moderate rate to 10 to 20 feet. Unsupported, the plant forms a shrubby ground cover. Its weakly twining stems need assistance to grow as a climbing vine. Try growing it against a fence as a backdrop for a bed of flowering perennials. Tied to an arbor or trellis, angel-wing jasmine makes a clean, attractive specimen plant. Or take advantage of its easy culture and place the vine in a container on a sunny patio. Angel-wing jasmine can also be used to trail over a bank or be placed among other plants as a low-growing accent vine.

Requirements for growing this easy-care plant are few. Provide a well-drained site, adding soil amendments to help lighten a heavy soil. Place in sun or partial shade and water regularly to keep the soil moist. A mulch aids water retention. Fertilize in early spring or summer with a balanced fertilizer. As the vine takes shape, pinch growing tips for increased flowering and bushiness. This vine tolerates heavy pruning and is easy to keep in bounds. Prune in fall after flowering or in early spring before active growth begins.

Jasminum polyanthum
Chinese Jasmine
Zones: 8-10.
Evergreen. Flowering.

Chinese jasmine is a vigorously growing vine reaching 20 feet. The plant is characterized by its finely divided leaves with 5 to 7 lance-shaped leaflets, which have a delicate, fine-textured appearance. Starlike blossoms will scent the garden for several months. In warm areas flowering begins in February and extends into summer. Flowers are white with rose-pink on the outside. They are held in dense clusters on side branches.

Its twining branches can cover a large fence or trellis and make a good ground cover for partially shaded areas. It is also well suited for container growing, and can be trained on a trellis in narrow spaces.

Chinese jasmine *(Jasminum polyanthum)* is vigorous; has fine-textured leaves. Clusters of wonderfully fragrant white flowers perfume the air for months. Flowers shown below.

Jasmines *(Jasminum sp.)* are easy-to-train evergreen vines. They require little care, and bear fragrant blossoms.

Flower buds of angel-wing jasmine *(Jasminum nitidum)* are purple-red; blossoms are bright white and fragrant when open.

Chinese jasmine has the same cultural requirements as angel-wing jasmine. It prefers a partly shaded location and regular watering during the growing season. Prune each year in fall after flowering to prevent branches from tangling and to control growth.

Lonicera

Honeysuckle

Honeysuckle vines can be found in historic gardens, growing wild in open and wooded areas, and in our modern landscapes. Most kinds have sweetly scented flowers that can fill the air with a heady fragrance on warm summer days. Hummingbirds are attracted to the nectar in honeysuckle flowers and many other birds feed on the berries.

Honeysuckle vines are rampant growers that need to be kept pruned or given room to roam. One type or another is adapted to almost every climate. They can be grown in a wide variety of soils and are relatively pest-free.

The following are three top-rated honeysuckles. Choose one to fit your needs and growing conditions for a lasting, dependable vine.

Lonicera hildebrandiana

Giant Burmese Honeysuckle

Zones: 9-10.

Evergreen. Flowering.

This vigorous vine is the largest of the honeysuckles, its twining, ropelike branches reaching lengths of 40 to 80 feet. Glistening, dark green leaves, 4 to 6 inches long, make an attractive background for the slender, tubular flowers. In summer, fragrant, 7-inch blossoms open creamy-white, fading to shades of yellow then gold before dropping. Small, dark green, berrylike fruits may appear in fall after the blooming season.

Giant Burmese honeysuckle is a vine for warm southern states of Zone 10 and has also proven reliable and popular in California gardens. Although its roots will sprout new growth after a freeze, it is best grown in regions where temperatures remain above 32°F. Provide shelter from strong winds.

A big, fast-growing vine, this honeysuckle needs a large area to spread, and the strong woody growth needs a sturdy support. Plant it to drape from tops of walls or grow along the eaves of a house. Espaliered against a fence, its large leaves and lovely flowers show to good advantage. Its fast growth and deep-rooting habit make it a very useful ground cover on slopes.

Giant Burmese honeysuckle grows in a wide range of soils. Soil should be kept evenly moist throughout the year. Occasional fertilizing keeps the vine looking healthy. Plant in full sun if near the coast or in partial shade in hot, inland areas. Prune the vine to remove or thin out old branches after blooms have faded.

Lonicera japonica

Japanese Honeysuckle

Zones: 4-10.

Evergreen or semideciduous.

Flowering.

Japanese honeysuckle is a heavily branched, rampant, climbing vine or ground cover best used in large gardens. Twining stems will quickly reach 15 to 30 feet. Leaves are evergreen in warm climates, semievergreen in cold climates. It is drought- and heat-tolerant, adapting to a wide range of climates. Sweetly scented flowers appear throughout the summer and attract bees. The flower buds are tinged purple and open white, aging to pale yellow. They are borne in pairs at the bases of the leaves, appearing as long, thin tubes with curled-back lips. Oval-shaped leaves are dark green, turning bronze with the onset of winter.

Japanese honeysuckle is a problem-solver for areas where other plants won't grow. It is not particular as to soil type and can be grown in poorly drained soils or on steep slopes. In some areas it is even considered a weed. In sun or shade, simply give it room to spread, or prune severely to control its growth.

Provide a support for it to twine around and it will grow upwards, or leave unsupported and stems will root to help stabilize hills and prevent erosion. It grows rapidly and will quickly cover a fence where a fragrant screen is desired.

Care for Japanese honeysuckle is primarily limited to controlling shape and size. Prune in fall or early spring. It responds well to both light and heavy pruning.

Three varieties are top-rated. 'Halliana', Hall's honeysuckle, has white flowers and green leaves and is the most vigorous and commonly grown variety. 'Gold-Net Honeysuckle' has distinctive yellow-marbled leaves, making it a good accent plant for the garden. It is less cold hardy and slower in growth rate than Hall's honeysuckle. 'Purple Japanese Honeysuckle' has a form similar to Hall's honeysuckle. Long flowers are tinged reddish purple, and leaves have purple undersides.

Lonicera sempervirens
Trumpet Honeysuckle
Zones: 4-10.
Evergreen or semideciduous.
Flowering.

Native to the eastern United States, this evergreen to semideciduous vine is well adapted to a broad range of climate zones. Trumpet honeysuckle makes a handsome, twining vine with an open form and coral to red flowers throughout the summer. Narrow, tubular blossoms are held at the ends of branches in showy clusters. They are not fragrant. Scarlet-colored fruit follow flowers in fall. Distinctive, broadly oval leaves have pale blue-green undersides and are joined to the stem at their bases.

This rampant-growing vine becomes shrubby if unsupported, making it a suitable ground cover for slopes and large areas. Used on a fence or trellis it forms an attractive screen. Provide sturdy support for the branches. Thin and cut back stems in early spring or after blooming. Pruning will control the size of the vine and encourage new branches.

Giant Burmese honeysuckle *(Lonicera hildebrandiana)* is a vigorous twining vine that needs plenty of space. Fragrant flowers shown below.

Japanese honeysuckle *(Lonicera japonica)*

Leaves of Boston ivy *(Parthenocissus tricuspidata)* turn brilliant scarlet and yellow in fall before dropping. The remaining network of branches creates an intricate and interesting pattern.

Like other honeysuckles, this vine is easy to grow and will tolerate sunny or shady exposures. It is adaptable to a wide variety of soils, preferring moist conditions for best growth. Watch for aphids on new growth.

If a yellow-flowered vine is what your garden needs, try the variety 'Sulphurea'. 'Superba' boasts bright, scarlet-colored flower clusters.

Parthenocissus

Virginia Creeper, Boston Ivy

Few vines can equal the dramatic fall color of Virginia creeper and Boston ivy, two top-rated vines of the grape family. Their leaves turn brilliant shades of red and gold, creating a dazzling autumn show. The vines climb with flat adhesive discs, borne at the ends of branching tendrils.

Use these vines to decorate sides of buildings or slopes where they can spread to cover large expanses. They are best on brick or stucco walls since they can damage shingles. Adaptable to a wide range of soils and climate zones, Virginia creeper and Boston ivy are popular vines for landscape use.

Parthenocissus quinquefolia
Virginia Creeper
Zones: 4-10.
Deciduous.

Virginia creeper is readily identified by its leaflets, which are arranged like fingers of a hand. There are 5 to a leaf, measuring 2 to 6 inches in length. They have coarsely toothed margins. When leaves appear in early spring, they are tinged purple, turning dark green as they mature, and shades of scarlet in the fall. Bluish-black berries on red stalks remain until winter when they drop to the ground or are eaten by birds.

Virginia creeper needs a rough surface to adhere to because its tendrils are less clinging than those of Boston ivy. Long drooping branches hang gracefully away from the vine. Use Virginia creeper to cover a trellis or fence, or the side of a building. Virginia creeper is also considered an excellent ground cover for slopes. Stems root where they touch ground and help stabilize soil.

This vine can grow in almost any garden setting, withstanding freezing temperatures or high summer heat, and it is drought-tolerant. It will grow in a wide range of soil types but a well-drained, loamy, moist soil is preferred. Grows well in sun or shade.

When planting new vines, place them close to their support and space about 2 to 4 feet apart for adequate coverage. Cut back stems in early stages of growth to induce branching. Guide branches up their support during the first year. Once established, the vine may be pruned in early spring to direct growth or keep it in bounds. When used as a ground cover, prune to encourage branching of stems. Watch for any leaf damage by Japanese beetles or leafhoppers. Mildew may be a problem in damp sites.

Two varieties of Virginia creeper are top-rated. Their smaller leaves create a softer effect when planted against a wall. 'Engelmannii', Engelmann creeper, forms a dense cover with small leathery leaves. 'Saint-Paulii', St. Paul's creeper, is a more tenacious clinger with rounder leaflets.

Parthenocissus tricuspidata
Boston Ivy
Zones: 4-10.
Deciduous.

There is no mistaking this vine when it displays its dramatic fall color, although at other times of the year it is sometimes confused with English ivy. In early fall the foliage changes to fiery shades of scarlet and yellow. An interesting meshwork of branches and persistent dark blue berries are left exposed after the leaves drop. Spring leaves are purplish when they first appear, maturing into large, green, 3-lobed leaves. They will eventually reach 8 inches in width. Individual leaves are held on long stems. They stand out from the branches and flutter gracefully in the breeze.

Boston ivy branches more and is a more tenacious climber than Virginia creeper. It will give good coverage over large expanses of wall. The vine branches from the base, spreading in all directions over its support. It is one of the best vines for city environments, tolerating dust and exhaust fumes. Use it to soften the appearance of exposed walls, especially those of city buildings or as a fence or ground cover.

Growing requirements for Boston ivy are similar to those of Virginia creeper. Widely adapted to many soil and climate conditions, the vine is slightly less cold tolerant, not growing quite as far north. Set Boston ivy in sun or shade and provide ample water during the growing season. Feed occasionally with a mild fertilizer, and watch for the same insect pests that bother Virginia creeper. To keep stems off windows and out of doorways, prune back branches before leaves appear in spring. Cut back old branches to their base to renew the vine.

The variety 'Lowii', Low's creeper, has deeply lobed 1-1/2-inch leaves on shorter stalks. Its growth is restrained, making it suitable for smaller areas. 'Veitchii', Veitch's creeper, has small, dainty leaves.

Boston ivy *(Parthenocissus tricuspidata)* clings to any surface with adhesive discs and can form a dense leafy cover on walls and buildings.

Virginia creeper *(Parthenocissus quinquefolia)*

Passiflora

Passionflower

Passionflower vines are native to South America, where they grow as tall clinging vines. In the United States they are grown primarily for their unique flowers, which bloom from spring through fall, and are used as a dense screening cover. In warmer climates, large edible fruit may be produced.

The name passionflower comes from a religious interpretation that

Purple granadilla *(Passiflora edulis)* quickly forms a dense screen over a wide area. Exotic flowers, shown below, bloom from June to September; edible fruits appear in spring and fall.

the distinctive flower parts are symbolic of the crucifixion of Christ. The sepals and petals represent the apostles, the stamens the wounds, the pistils the nails, and a filamentous corona the halo or thorny crown. These flower parts have contrasting colors, which add to the blossom's beauty.

Gardeners in warm winter climates will find this rampant grower an easy vine to cultivate. It tolerates arid conditions as well as coastal environments. With protection from freezing temperatures, its range can be extended farther north into Zone 7, where it will be deciduous.

Some varieties will reach 40 feet, climbing with clinging corkscrew-like tendrils. Numerous branches, thickly covered with large, deeply lobed leaves, are quite ornamental.

Passionflower vines require a large area in which to grow. They are often used for cascading wall covers or shading on patios. Rooting branches can be effective as a stabilizing ground cover on banks. In cold climates it's an exotic vine for growing in the greenhouse.

Passionflower grows in a variety of soil types. Regular watering and fertilizing produces best growth. Place in the sunniest spot in the garden. Where temperatures are cool, the plant should be held against a south- or west-facing wall to take advantage of reflected heat.

Passionflower is a vigorous grower and will need a sturdy framework for support. It usually requires heavy pruning each year to remove old branches and control the rampant growth. Remove stems at their origin to open up the vine.

Caterpillars are the most serious pest of passionflower vine. They frequently chew leaves.

Passiflora x alatocaerulea

Hybrid Passionflower

Zones: 9-10.

Evergreen or semievergreen.

Flowering.

This hybridized vine is the most popular of the passionflowers because of its large flowers and pest resistance.

Three-inch-long leaves have 3 lance-shaped lobes with smooth margins. Long-lasting, fragrant flowers have white sepals and pink petals with green undersides that form a star-shaped outer ring. The showy filaments or corona are tipped white with blue centers and purple bases. No fruit forms.

Display this vine against a warm wall, drape it from a strong trellis, or use as a patio cover. Mulch roots for maximum cold tolerance.

Passiflora caerulea

Blue Passionflower

Zones: 9-10.

Evergreen or semievergreen.

Flowering.

Blue passionflower is one of the most vigorous species. Its slender, intertwining stems grow to 40 feet. Leaves are deeply divided, have narrow lobes, and are smaller than those of the hybrid passionflower. Blossoms are 3 to 4 inches across and have white to pale pink sepals and petals. The corona is deep purple at the base, tipped white.

Blue passionflower can be used as an upright vine or spreading ground cover. Provide a large growing space. Heavy pruning will keep it in bounds and reduce the massive growth. Watch for caterpillar damage.

Two cultivars are available: 'Constance' has lovely, pure white flowers and 'Grandiflora' boasts 5- to 6-inch blossoms.

Passiflora edulis

Purple Granadilla, Passion Fruit

Zones: 9-10.

Semievergreen. Flowering.

Purple granadilla is a woody climber grown mainly for its exotic, edible fruit. The vine can cover a large area to form a thick screen. Dark green, shiny foliage completely covers the vine to its full height of 30 feet. Leaves can be identified by their 3-parted lobes with coarsely toothed margins. White flowers marked with purple, borne from June to September, are 2 to 3 inches across.

Fruits form in spring and fall. They are 2 to 3 inches long and egg-shaped, with a hard, dark purple rind when ripe. A long, warm growing season improves fruit quality. Vines bear fruit in their second year. Prune back branches to encourage flowering and control the size.

Polygonum aubertii

Silver Lace Vine

Zones: 5-10.
Evergreen or deciduous.
Flowering.

This profusely blooming vine is named for its billowy, small flowers that blanket the tops of its branches. Silver lace vine, also called fleece flower in some regions, blooms from late summer to midfall, when most other plants have finished flowering. Greenish-white blossoms are held in dense, upright clusters above the stems. Distinctive, arrow-shaped leaves, 1-1/2 to 2 inches long, have wavy margins and glossy surfaces. New leaves appear pale green with red tips. Grows rapidly to 15 to 30 feet and makes a quick cover for a fence or arbor. The vine is deciduous in cold winter areas and evergreen in mild climates.

Silver lace vine is an excellent accent plant for use in tough growing conditions. Thrives in heavy or sandy soils and requires only occasional fertilizing. The vine is partially drought-tolerant. Monthly deep waterings keep the plant healthy during the summer growing season. In cold climates, the top of the plant may die to the ground in winter, but hardy roots will send up new shoots in spring.

Silver lace vine is the plant to choose for sites where other vines would suffer from rigors of strong winds or adverse city conditions. It is also relatively pest-free.

Silver lace vine takes full sun in most areas, partial shade in areas with hot summers. Newly established plants will need branches tied to a support for early training. Thereafter, thin and guide branches to

From late summer to midfall, silver lace vine *(Polygonum aubertii)* wears a dainty shawl of billowy blooms. Forms a quick cover for fence or arbor in difficult growing conditions. Flowers shown below.

Cape grape *(Rhoicissus capensis)* has a graceful, airy habit, shiny green leaves. Bears small edible fruits.

'Climbing Cecile Brunner' *(Rosa sp.)* is one of many spectacular roses available in climbing form.

maintain an attractive form. Pinch growing tips to increase bushiness. Branches pruned in fall are quickly replaced the following season. Mid-spring pruning will help control the shape of the vine, however flowering will be delayed.

When a light fence cover is desired, silver lace vine makes a splendid choice. Stems twine quickly over their support. Creates a lovely effect on a pergola or as a patio cover. At its best shown cascading over tops of walls. In bloom, the frothy flowers look like white foam.

Rhoicissus capensis (Cissus capensis)

Cape Grape, Evergreen Grape

Zone: 10.
Evergreen.

Cape grape is a handsome vine with large, roundish to kidney-shaped leaves. Rusty-colored hairs on the undersides of leaves and bronzy new growth give added visual interest. Plant form is similar to that of its relative the edible grape. Long, branched tendrils cling to fences and lattice-work to form a dense, lush green cover. The vine can reach up to 30 feet. It bears small, 1/2-inch, edible berries. Although primarily planted for their ornamental value, the glossy reddish-black fruit can be used in cooking and preserves. Flowers appear in spring but are not ornamental.

Cape grape is a vine for warm climate areas where frost is rare. Large leaves make it an excellent shade plant for patio or veranda. Provide strong support for its long branches. On a trellis, leaves create an attractive landscape accent. Drape the vine over a tall fence or send it cascading down a bank. Give it a large area to grow in. Cape grape, and many of its relatives in the grape family, are popular houseplants that tolerate low light. Grows outdoors in shade.

The vine grows from large, 6- to 8-inch tubers, which do best in a rich, well-drained soil. They withstand somewhat dry conditions but flourish when kept moist and mulched. This is particularly beneficial when growing the vine in hot climates. Protect from prolonged freezing.

Cape grape is a moderate- to slow-growing vine. Young plants should be guided where you want them to grow. Pinch tips of branches for a bushy plant and thin to control size. Prune in early spring or fall.

Mealybugs can be a pest in the garden or indoors. Watch for the characteristic cottony masses on stems and undersides of leaves. Control by hosing them off the plant or using the appropriate insecticide.

Rosa

Climbing Rose

Zones: 5-10.
Deciduous. Flowering.

Climbing roses bring incomparable elegance and beauty to a garden. They grace building eaves, add drama to a fence or post, or create a romantic arch over an arbor or trellis. Flower color and fragrance in climbing roses is as diverse as in shrub forms.

Climbing roses do not actually twine or cling; their long branches must be trained and tied to a support. An unsupported vine can look attractive in a large landscape where it will form a sprawling, mounded shrub. Some kinds grow only to 10 feet long, others reach 50 feet.

Basically, there are 3 types of climbing roses: large-flowered climbers, climbing sports, and ramblers. Large-flowered climbers have canes that are stout, stiff, and grow from 8 to 15 feet high. Flowers are 2 to 6 inches across and borne in open clusters of up to 25 blossoms. Vines reach their bloom peak in spring but continue to flower throughout the season.

Large-flowered climbers are the best choice for cold winter areas where temperatures do not drop below −18°F. They are the most cold hardy of climbing roses and are relatively pest-free.

The second type of climbing rose is called a climbing sport. They are created by propagating exceptionally long vigorous canes that form spontaneously on normal bush roses. The prized flowers of the bush form are also produced by the climber. Although blooming less prolifically than large-flowered climbers, climbing sports offer a fine form and high quality flowers. Climbing sports are hardy to 20°F. Tipping the plant over and completely covering it in late fall with a protective mulch will help it withstand winter temperatures as low as −10°F.

Varieties of climbing sports are named for the bush rose from which they were developed, because they have the same flower and fragrance characteristics. Look for the popular shrub name preceded by the word "climbing" to select the rose variety of your choice.

A few of the best-loved varieties available include: 'Climbing Cecile Brunner', small pink flowers; 'Climbing Charlotte Armstrong', pink flowers; 'Climbing Chrysler Imperial', red flowers; 'Climbing First Prize', pink flowers; 'Climbing Mrs. Sam McGrady', orange flowers; 'Climbing Peace', yellow flowers; and 'Climbing Snowbird', white flowers.

Other long-caned roses suitable for climbing include the ramblers. They are hardy to −10°F, if protected. The old-fashioned Lady Banks' rose, *Rosa banksiae*, is included in this group, as are 'Evangeline' with pink single blossoms in profusion, and 'Chevy Chase' with small red flowers. Blooms are produced in abundance on 1-year-old canes. Ramblers have supple canes growing to over 20 feet. They need a yearly pruning to remove old wood and make room for younger flowering canes. When canes are supported, ramblers make a good cover for the sides of tall fences or buildings. Trailing types such as 'Dorothy Perkins' or 'May Queen' grow low, and form colorful ground covers.

Lady Banks' rose *(Rosa banksiae)* is a long-time favorite rambler. It is very hardy and widely grown as a cover for tall fences or buildings.

Climbing roses *(Rosa sp.)* 'Climbing Peace' (left) and 'Joseph's Coat' (right) are dramatic and colorful garden accents.

Cape honeysuckle *(Tecomaria capensis),* shown above and below, forms a luxurious dense screen. Flowers available in many colors.

Cape honeysuckle *(Tecomaria capensis)* bears colorful flowers summer through fall.

Climbing roses will grow and blossom with a minimum of care. With extra attention they can be the pride of the garden. Treat climbing roses as you would shrub roses. They grow best in a soil rich in organic matter. Select a sunny location with good air circulation for healthy-looking leaves and prolific flowering. Apply a top mulch for water conservation and weed control. Water deeply and regularly during the growing season. Fertilize in early spring and after flowering.

Prune climbing roses to remove old and dead wood, control growth, and increase flower production. Large-flowered climbers form buds on 6- to 12-inch laterals of 2- to 3-year-old canes. Shorten these laterals to 3 to 6 inches or 3 or 4 buds in early spring before bud break. Remove faded flowers in summer on varieties that bloom repeatedly to encourage further flowering. Removal of spent blossoms also discourages seed formation. Renew and shape the plant by removing oldest canes.

Climbing sports should be secured to their support and allowed to grow unpruned until the desired height is achieved. Then direct growth by bending canes over a fence or trellis. Flowers will be produced in greater quantities on these horizontal branches and they will continue to form buds for several years. For larger flowers remove lateral branches and cut back flowering shoots to 3 or 4 inches.

Pests occur, even on the best-maintained roses. With a good program for control, plants can remain healthy and thriving. Watch for signs of damage caused by aphids, powdery mildew, blackspot, leafhoppers, mites, and rust.

Tecomaria capensis

Cape Honeysuckle

Zones: 9-10.
Evergreen. Flowering.

Cape honeysuckle is a vigorous, rambling, shrubby vine that is widely grown from Southern California to Florida. Brilliant red flowers make a striking show in the landscape. It is often planted on hot, dry banks where it forms an effective ground cover, spreading 8 to 10 feet, or used against exposed rock walls. Supported on a fence, cape honeysuckle takes the shape of a dense shrubby vine and will create a finely textured, deep green screen. Long, flexible stems can be tied to a support for an espalier or trellis cover.

The long, slender branches of cape honeysuckle bear shiny, dark green leaves that are divided into small leaflets, creating a delicate lacy effect. Borne 5 to 9 on a stem, leaflets are oval with toothed margins. Flowers appear in late summer and blooming continues through fall. Fiery orange-red flowers are held out from the foliage in upright, terminal clusters. Funnel-shaped blossoms are 2 inches long, with red protruding stamens. For yellow flowers plant the variety 'Aurea'. Its growth is less vigorous and it is not as cold-tolerant as the red-flowered form.

Cape honeysuckle is a tough plant. It thrives in hot sun and tolerates windy, coastal conditions. Grows in partial shade but will produce fewer flowers. Recovers from light frosts. In cold inland valleys protective measures will extend its range.

Flowers are borne on new growth. For best results cut back stems in late fall and winter after blossoming. Can be pruned successfully throughout the year to shape and control growth. Thin branches if they become too dense.

Cape honeysuckle can be grown in sandy- or clay-textured soils as long as there is adequate drainage. It prefers a moist soil but once established can tolerate periods of dryness. Cape honeysuckle is relatively pest-free.

Trachelospermum

Star Jasmine

The sweet fragrance of its flowers and the clean, neat appearance of its foliage make star jasmine a top-rated vine for the landscape. Two- to three-inch star-shaped flowers cover the plant from late April to July, and contrast nicely against the glossy, dark green foliage. Supple branches criss-cross and twine to form a vine, ground cover, or sprawling shrub.

Star jasmine is a versatile evergreen plant that can satisfy a variety of garden needs. It is an excellent choice for trellis-work along a narrow walkway. In sun or shade, the dense foliage will create an effective, all-season screen. Supported over a small patio or entryway, its enchanting scent can be enjoyed for months. As a ground cover, star jasmine becomes a thick green carpet suitable on banks, near walkways, and under tall shrubs. It makes a lovely cascading shrub for raised planters.

Although slow to start, star jasmine becomes a moderately fast-growing vine. Upright, it will reach over 15 feet. As a ground cover, growth will be more restrained, spreading 4 to 5 feet with a height of 1-1/2 to 2 feet.

Star jasmines are vines for mild climates of the Atlantic Coast, Gulf Coast and western states. In hot, sunny climates, place the vine in filtered sun. In cooler coastal areas grow in full sun. The vine tolerates windy conditions.

Star jasmines enjoy a moist, well-drained site but are not too particular about soil type. An application of fertilizer in early spring and late summer will encourage good green foliage color and enthusiastic growth. Water regularly through spring and summer months. Keep the plant moderately moist.

Maintenance of star jasmine is easy. When buying new plants to be grown as upright vines, select plants with long branches. Tie branches to a sturdy support for early training. Prune long branches during any season to help the vine hold its shape. Shear vines covering fences in early spring or fall to keep them neat and trim. Mature vines should be pruned annually to encourage new branches and to eliminate

Yellow star jasmine *(Trachelospermum asiaticum)* is easily trained and maintained. Plant to frame an entryway, as a ground cover, or fence screen.

Star jasmine *(Trachelospermum jasminoides)* bears intensely fragrant white flowers from late spring into summer.

Star jasmine *(Trachelospermum jasminoides)* is a versatile landscape vine that doubles as ground cover.

Star jasmine *(Trachelospermum jasminoides)* performs well in many landscape situations; bears fragrant flowers.

older, woody branches. Star jasmine is relatively pest-free but can be bothered by aphids, mealybugs, red spider mites or scale.

Trachelospermum asiaticum
Yellow Star Jasmine
Zones: 7-10.
Evergreen. Flowering.

Yellow star jasmine is a handsome plant native to Japan. It is less vigorous than the white-flowered star jasmine, but is a good choice for the colder climate Zones of 7 and 8.

Light yellow fragrant flowers are borne in slender terminal clusters with their wavy petals held erect. They are showy from April through June. Leaves differ from its white-flowered counterpart. They are darker in color, broader, with a dull surface. New growth is colored bronze.

This plant makes a handsome, restrained ground cover, fence screen, or plant for hanging baskets, indoors or out.

Trachelospermum jasminoides
Star Jasmine, Confederate Jasmine
Zones: 8-10.
Evergreen. Flowering.

Although white-flowered star jasmine is native to China, it is one of the most commonly grown vines in the United States. It is an extremely popular plant in the South and West, having been grown for so long in the southern United States it has been given the common name of confederate jasmine. It is a more vigorous grower than yellow star jasmine, reaching 20 feet when supported.

Star jasmine's dark green leaves are very attractive, with a glossy surface and simple oval shape. Lacy, star-shaped flowers have twisted petals on short tubes. The fragrant blossoms open in early May, lasting until midsummer. Its sweet flowers are filled with nectar, attracting bees to the garden.

Use to cover arbors, patios, or as a screen for small gardens. Drape over walls and raised planters for a trailing effect. To establish as a ground cover, space plants 2 to 3 feet apart for dense coverage. Cut back long branches to encourage denser growth.

The leaves of 'Variegatum' have green and white variegations, often tinged with red. It is hardier than its parent.

Vitis
Grape

Grape vines are all-season performers. Grapes are top-rated because of their abundant fruit production, lush foliage, colorful fall leaves, and interesting bare branches. Some varieties are grown purely for their foliage and ornamental effect. Others not only decorate the landscape, but are highly valued for their fruit, which is used for raisins, wine, juice, and eating fresh.

Native American grape vines, such as *V. labrusca* and *V. riparia* species, are the most cold hardy. American varieties have splendid fall color; their fruit has a delicious flavor.

Varieties of the European grape, *V. vinifera,* are generally used in areas with a long, warm growing season. They are hardy to 10°F and used in Zones 7 to 10. European grapes are grown in California for table grapes and wine production.

Many hybrids between American and European grape varieties exist that have intermediate climate adaptation. They are called French hybrids and include many useful varieties such as 'Aurora', 'Baco #1', and 'Seyve Villard 12-375'.

Grape vines grow with great vigor, putting on several feet of new growth in a season. They are excellent plants to grow on a lattice over a patio. Long, compact clusters of colorful fruit hang below the foliage. If fruit is not harvested, a cleanup will be needed. Grape leaves are quite large, up to 12 inches across, and make a good shady cover or interesting espalier against a wall.

Vines require training and attachment to supports. Branches can be held on a trellis of heavy wire or laid flat over the top of an arbor. Once established, grape plants have deep roots. They prefer well-drained soils that are slightly alkaline but adapt to other conditions. Fertilizing will encourage leaf and stem growth but does not increase fruit production. Grape clusters will be larger and leaves healthier if plants are given ample water.

Some varieties have high heat requirements, and plants should be grown in full sun. Planting against a warm south- or west-facing wall will help in cooler climates.

There are two basic types of grape vine pruning. Spur pruning is most used on the fruiting European vines to encourage grape production. Canes are cut back in winter to 2 or 3 buds. These buds will produce fruiting canes. Some thinning of branches can be done for ornamental purposes. Height is achieved by increasing the point at which canes branch.

Cane pruning is primarily used on American varieties. Canes are cut back to 6 to 18 buds, and trained to a trellis or lead wire. Pruning is done in fall.

Mildew is a common problem of grape vines; dust with sulphur during the growing season to control.

When selecting vines for the garden, consult local references to determine the best variety for your area. Many varieties are suited to specific localities and extend the range in which grapes can be grown. Consider cold hardiness, heat requirement, time needed to ripen fruit, fruit size and quality.

Vitis labrusca
Fox Grape, American Grape
Zones: 6-10.
Deciduous.

These are slip-skin grapes used for table and juice. Vines are cold-tolerant to 0°F and are a good choice where the growing season is short and cool. The fruits have a strong flavor, typified by Concord grapes. Popular American grape varieties include 'Catawba', 'Delaware', 'Fredonia', 'Himrod', 'Niagara', 'Seneca', and 'Steuben'.

Grapes *(Vitis sp.)* are vigorous vines that can be trained to fit neatly into small spaces, as used in the landscape above, or left unrestrained to cover arbors or other structures, such as the bridge shown below.

Grape vines *(Vitis sp.)* cast light shade, have colorful fall foliage, and bear beautiful clusters of delicious fruit, shown below.

Vitis rotundifolia
Muscadine Grape, Scuppernong
Zones: 8-10.
Deciduous.

This grape grows wild in the southern United States. It thrives in hot, humid weather. Small fruits have a strong musky aroma. Vines are vigorous. Many varieties have been chosen that have localized adaptation to different parts of the South. Check with your local nurseryman for adaptation of varieties such as 'Bountiful', 'Carlos', 'Higgins', 'Hunt', and 'Southland'.

Vitis vinifera
European Grape
Zones: 7-10.
Deciduous.

The fruits are tight-skinned and mild-flavored, making high quality grapes for wine and table. They are most commonly grown in California because they require a long, frost-free period with warm temperatures. European grapes are also grown in the Pacific Northwest and sometimes in Arizona. These vines are hardy to 10°F. 'Ribier', 'Thompson Seedless', and 'Muscat' are familiar table grapes good for the home garden. Popular wine grape varieties include: 'Cabernet Sauvignon', 'Chardonnay', 'Chenin Blanc', and 'Zinfandel'.

Wisteria
Wisteria

Abundant blossoms on gracefully cascading stems make wisteria one of the most prized vines for the landscape. Old vines are especially appreciated for their grand size and woody, twisting trunks. A vigorous grower suitable for a broad range of climate zones, wisteria can grow from the cold North and Midwest to the warmest western states.

Large compound leaves look delicate and have small, oval leaflets, 7 to 9 on a stem. Their light green color is bright and appealing when draped over a patio. Dramatic clusters of pealike blossoms are borne in early spring. Color varies from a clear white, to pink and shades of violet. Flowers hang in long pendulous clusters measuring from 6 inches to 4 feet. Velvety seed pods, 3 to 6 inches long, follow.

Wisteria makes an attractive garden specimen or handsome twining cover for a fence, arbor, pergola, or patio. It's best not to grow wisteria against a wooden house because the strong vines can damage shingles. The beauty of its flowers and delicate tracery of its leaves add a sense of elegance to any garden. Japanese landscapes have traditionally placed wisteria to reflect in a pool of water.

Wisteria will need a sturdy frame to support its heavy, twining branches. If trained for a small area, the woody branches can eventually support their own weight. A small, graceful tree form can be attained if the woody stem is trained to a single trunk at an early age.

To ensure prolific flowering, choose selected varieties. Plants grown from seed can take up to 15 years to bloom and will vary in flower color. Pruning wisteria after flowering, or in the winter, will reduce vegetative growth and encourage spring bloom. Prune with care when the branches are bare. Shorten long branches to within 3 to 5 buds. Pruning can also be done after blossoming in early summer to limit the number of vigorous stems and create an attractive framework.

A loamy, moist soil is ideal for wisteria. It will perform well under a wide range of conditions with adequate drainage and ample water during the growing season. Iron chlorosis may develop in alkaline soils. To encourage blossoming, fertilize in early spring with superphosphate fertilizer before bud break.

Vines listed below are two of nine recognized wisteria species. They are from East Asia and have gained the widest use in the landscape.

Wisteria floribunda
Japanese Wisteria
Zones: 5-9.
Deciduous. Flowering.

The blossoms of Japanese wisteria open sequentially from the top of its cluster to the bottom. Although the length of its blooming period is longer than that of Chinese wisteria, Japanese wisteria does not burst into bloom with the dramatic impact of its Chinese relative. The flower clusters measure from 8 to 48 inches in length. All varieties are pleasantly fragrant with flowers in shades of white, pink, and violet. Japanese wisteria is the hardier of the two species. Plant in full sun. Following are a few of the more than 40 recognized varieties:

'Alba', white flowers on 1-1/2- to 2-foot stems; 'Issai', 12-inch blue-violet clusters; 'Violacea Plena', a purple, double-flowered form; 'Rosea', fragrant pink flowers; 'Macrobotrys', purple-blue flowers on stalks up to 3 feet long; 'Longissima', with the longest flower clusters reaching 4 feet under ideal conditions.

Wisteria sinensis
Chinese Wisteria
Zones: 5-9.
Deciduous. Flowering.

This is the wisteria most often seen in American gardens. Its blue-violet flowers open simultaneously in dense clusters 6 to 12 inches long.

Slightly fragrant blossoms appear from April to May, just before the leaves emerge. The number and size of leaflets help distinguish this species from *W. floribunda,* the Japanese wisteria. Leaves of Chinese wisteria have 7 to 13 leaflets that are 2 to 3 inches long. Japanese wisteria has 13 to 19 shorter leaflets.

Three varieties are available. 'Alba' has white fragrant flowers. 'Purpurea' is the familiar violet-colored variety. 'Plena' has double flowers.

Other species of wisteria with horticultural value include:

W. x formosa, a fragrant hybrid of Chinese and Japanese wisteria. Flowers open simultaneously. *W. macrostachya,* Kentucky wisteria, is the showiest of North American species. *W. venusta,* silky wisteria, is characterized by the velvety surface of leaves, and fragrant white flowers. Its variety 'Violacea' has violet flowers.

Graceful clusters of wisteria blossoms *(Wisteria sp.)* welcome spring with their sweet perfume. Solid support such as the sturdy arbor above, or fence shown below, is required to hold up the heavy branches.

Caring for Vines

Though vines are vigorous, enthusiastic growers, you need to get them off to a good start in your garden. Proper soil preparation, appropriate planting and pruning techniques, and regular watering are essential for establishing a new vine.

Preplanting Care

Vines are sold at nurseries in three forms: bareroot, balled-and-burlapped, and in containers.

Bareroot: These are field-grown, deciduous vines that are dug up while dormant and handled with little or no soil around the roots, hence the term "bareroot".

Some plants are available bareroot in fall as soon as leaves drop. Most are available in late winter or early spring once soil is workable and planting can begin. Vines that you order from a mail-order nursery may be bareroot. They are shipped to you at the best spring planting time for your area.

If selecting bareroot vines at the local nursery, look for ones with good-sized, well balanced roots. Lateral roots should radiate from the main root in several directions on several levels. Buds should be plump and firm, not dried up.

If you cannot plant a bareroot vine right away, dig a shallow trench or hole in a shaded part of the garden. Lay the roots in the trench and cover them with moist soil. (Horticulture jargon for this process is "heeling-in".) If weather is cool, bareroot vines can be safely heeled-in for up to 2 weeks. But if weather is warming and buds begin to swell, plant the vines immediately.

At left: Star jasmine *(Trachelospermum jasminoides)* is a garden favorite in temperate regions. Evergreen, with fragrant flowers and handsome glossy foliage.

Japanese honeysuckle *(Lonicera sp.)*

Trumpet creeper *(Campsis sp.)*

Creeping fig *(Ficus pumila)*

Grape *(Vitis sp.)*

Balled-and-burlapped: Vines that do not tolerate bareroot treatment are commonly offered balled-and-burlapped. Like bareroot vines, these plants are field-grown, but they are dug with a ball of soil left around their roots. Soil and roots are usually wrapped in burlap.

Container-grown: These plants have been grown in the metal or plastic container in which you buy them. Available throughout the growing season, container-grown vines can be planted anytime, even while in full flower. In fact, it is a good idea to shop for the vine you want during the flowering season. Individual plants, even of the same species, vary, and seeing them in flower is the only sure way of getting the flowering habit and color you want.

When selecting a container plant, it pays to be aware of plants to avoid. Don't choose the smallest or largest in the group. If the smallest is small due to weak and slow growth, whatever the causes, it will most likely continue with weak growth. Large plants have too much top growth compared to root growth—what experts call a low root-to-top ratio. These vines are likely to suffer excessive shock upon planting.

Containers are usually plastic or metal. Most nursery personnel will offer to cut the sides of metal containers. While this makes planting easier, it is recommended *only if you are sure you can plant the same day.* Once cans are cut the rootball dries out quickly. Press the cut container together and tie with twine to help slow moisture loss.

Many containers are made of dark-colored materials, which when exposed to full sun can heat up rapidly to root-damaging temperatures. Shade containers with a board, mounded soil, or low wall.

Soil

Soil texture, drainage, and pH (acid-alkaline balance) should be considered when you select and plant a vine.

Soil texture: Texture is determined by the relative quantities of sand, silt, and clay. Soils that are mostly sand have limited water and nutrient reserves but permit generous quantities of air to circulate around roots. Clay soils, by contrast, have plenty of water and nutrient capacity but restrict air. Neither type of soil is necessarily bad but it helps to be aware of their characteristic limitations.

Adding plenty of organic matter, such as composted bark or sawdust, peat moss or leafmold, is the best way to improve either clay or sand soils. In extremely sandy or clay soils, make planting holes twice as wide as otherwise recommended and amend the backfill soil to be a gradual transition to your garden's soil.

Soil drainage: Check drainage before planting by filling the planting hole with water and letting it drain. Refill the hole with water and time how long it takes to drain. Water should drain at about one-quarter inch per hour. If drainage is too slow, you can improve it by boring through restrictive soil layers with an auger or posthole digger, then fill the bored hole with amended soil. You may want to avoid poor-draining soil entirely by planting in raised beds or mounds.

Soil pH: Chemists measure soil acidity and alkalinity on the pH scale. It ranges from 0 to 14, with the low numbers indicating acidity and the high numbers alkalinity. The midpoint, 7, is neutral.

Most vines prefer a slightly acid soil pH, measuring between 6 and 7 on the scale. Boston ivy prefers acid soil; clematis grows best in alkaline soil.

If planting adjacent to a recently constructed wall or home foundation, clear away all concrete and mortar debris. These materials are strongly alkaline and might retard growth of some vines.

Soil pH may vary from garden to garden but generally is determined by the amount of rainfall an area receives. Rain washes natural limestone from soil, increasing its acidity. Areas of high rainfall have the most acid soil; areas of low rainfall have alkaline soil.

East of Columbus, Ohio; Lexington, Kentucky; Nashville, Tennessee; Jackson, Mississippi; and New Orleans, Louisiana is usually very acid soil. Westward from those cities in an almost straight line north-to-south between eastern Minnesota and Houston, Texas, soils are moderately acidic.

The Plains States to the Sierra Nevadas tend to be alkaline. West of the Cascade Mountains including northwestern California, western Oregon, and western Washington, soils are again very acid.

You can measure the pH of your garden soil by using one of the simple test kits available at most garden centers. Or, ask your local county agricultural extension office about university or private laboratory soil tests.

To raise the pH from 5.5 to 6.5, add ground dolomite limestone, 4 to 8 pounds per 100 square feet. Use less in sandy soil, more in clay soil. Limestone is slow-acting so apply it 1 or 2 months before planting, if possible.

Add sulfur, iron sulfate, and organic matter to lower a high pH. Sulfur at 2 pounds per 100 square feet will gradually reduce pH from 7.5 to 6.5. About 4 pounds of iron sulfate per 100 square feet has an equivalent effect. Organic matter of any kind will gradually increase soil acidity as it decomposes.

Planting

The best time to plant bareroot vines is late winter or early spring. In the North this means as soon as the soil can be worked. The term "bareroot season" in the South and West signals arrival of bareroot plants at the nurseries. In general, you can plant bareroot vines anytime they are dormant, late fall to late winter.

Balled-and-burlapped or container-grown vines can be planted in spring or fall. Where soil freezes,

Soil

Clay soil has smooth texture and retains moisture.

Sandy soil is gritty, loose, and fast-draining.

Loam soil combines the best features of clay and sandy soils.

Planting

1. Mix organic amendment into garden soil to make backfill mix.

2. Add backfill to planting hole to a depth of about 8 inches.

3. Add water to planting hole to moisten and settle backfill.

4. Loosen roots that the container has forced to coil or circle, and set rootball in planting hole.

5. Add backfill around rootball, firming with your hands. Fasten twining stems to support with garden ties, if needed.

6. Be sure the original rootball receives ample water the first year after planting.

plant vines early in fall to give them ample time to root before severe winter weather. Then apply a 2- to 3-inch layer of organic mulch (fir bark or composted sawdust, for example) to slow penetration of cold into the soil and to prevent heaving, the repeated freezing and thawing of soil that can break roots.

In the South where soil does not freeze, balled-and-burlapped and container-grown vines are planted throughout the winter. If you plant in winter, keep in mind that new plants need regular watering even though temperatures are low and that new plants in exposed, windy locations need protection from strong, drying winds.

TRAINING AND SUPPORTING

Initially young non-clinging vines may need some help in growing up the support you provide. Common garden ties may be used to fasten twining branches to the support. Often simply wrapping the branch around the support is sufficient to get it started coiling upward. Information on the types of support appropriate for different varieties of vines is included in the encyclopedia entries, and in the landscaping section.

SPACING

Spacing of vines is based upon the particular plant's spread, rate of growth, and the density of growth you desire. One wisteria or Boston ivy will eventually cover the side of a house. But if you want a fast, dense cover along a fence, space plants about 5 feet apart. Space particularly fast growers, such as wisteria, more widely; space slow growers, such as euonymus, more closely.

THE PLANTING HOLE

Balled-and-burlapped and container-grown plants require a hole depth equal to their rootball depth. A hole of adequate width is some 5 to 8 inches wider than the rootball. Bareroot plants should also be planted at their original nursery depth, though sometimes that level is difficult to determine. If you look closely at the bark just above the root system, you'll notice the proper soil level is indicated by a change in bark color—lighter below ground level and darker above. Once you locate the proper soil level on the trunk, mark it with string or tape. Plant bareroot vines by spreading the roots over a low cone of soil in the center of the hole.

It is better to have the hole too shallow than too deep. Loose soil in a deep hole will settle after planting until your vine is lower than you intend. Planted too deeply, surface roots suffocate and the portion of the trunk not adapted to burial may be attacked by disease organisms. Clematis is an important exception. It benefits by being planted 2 to 4 inches deeper than the original nursery depth.

"Backfill" is gardener's shorthand for the soil that is returned to the planting hole after the plant is properly situated. The best backfill is the garden soil you dug out in the first place. However, keep in mind the need for proper transition. Distinct layers of unlike soils create barriers to water movement and hence, root growth. If you are planting a bareroot vine, backfill with native soil. But if planting a container-grown vine, the ideal backfill is a half-and-half mixture of the container soil and your garden soil. Most likely you will not have a supply of the grower's container mix, so instead use a good organic material such as compost, milled or shredded peat moss, or composted wood by-products.

HOW TO PLANT

After you determine the correct hole depth, try the plant in the hole, adjusting it in various directions until the most attractive side faces the most frequent viewpoint.

Remember, do not cut metal containers until the planting day. Lift container plants carefully from the rootball, not the lower trunk.

On balled-and-burlapped vines, untie the burlap covering once most of the backfill is in place and spread it over the soil. The burlap will eventually rot. A wood-fiber container will also rot, but tear away the 1 or 2 inches that protrudes above soil level.

Pruning and planting: Pruning at this time is especially important for bareroot and balled-and-burlapped vines. These plants have been field-dug and lost many roots in the process. Prune top growth to compensate for lost roots. Many nurseries will cut back bareroot plants for you.

It is also a good idea to prune container-grown vines after planting. It is not unusual to damage a few roots during transplanting. In fact, some gardeners recommend purposefully trimming container plant rootballs in order to stimulate new root growth away from the tight circular pattern caused by the container.

Always remove any dead or broken branches. Cut away about one-third of young, healthy branches to maintain the plant's attractive, natural proportions. Make cuts just above buds (found where leaf stem joins branches) that point in the direction you want subsequent growth to take.

Watering

New vines, no matter how drought-tolerant once established, need regular watering their first season. After planting, make a low basin with loose soil around the plant to hold water. Make the basin just slightly larger than the vine's original balled-and-burlapped or container-grown rootball. It is very important—especially at first—for the rootball to be thoroughly soaked with each watering. It is an unfortunate but common experience for a careful gardener to watch a new plant die of drought despite conscientious watering. When the texture of the rootball and garden soil is different, the garden soil sometimes soaks up water but the plant's rootball remains dry.

Watering

Drip watering systems are efficient. They apply water directly over roots at a rate soil can absorb.

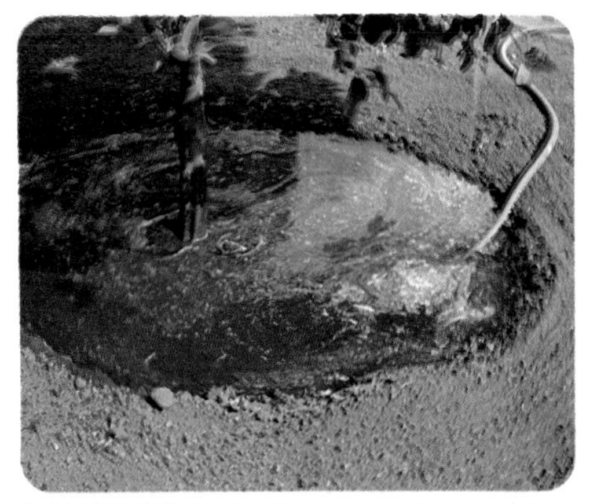

A basin of firmed soil directs water to roots—however periodic repair is required.

Many types of sprinklers are available for use on your garden hose. Easily moved where needed.

Mulching

Rock mulch does not wash away and lasts indefinitely, but does not add humus to soil.

Bark mulch is available in many sizes. Use uniform-size particles to give plantings a neat appearance.

Wooden boards laid in neat patterns on top of garden soil make an effective and visually pleasing type of mulch.

Fertilizing

Time-release pellets provide nutrients for 1 to 5 years. Read product directions.

Granular fertilizer applied on surface can promote good growth. Do not apply directly on rootball of vine.

Spray leaves with foliar fertilizer for fastest results.

Drip watering systems are excellent for widely spaced vines. Many varieties of drip watering systems are available. Most are a combination of small diameter plastic tubing and "emitters", small valves that allow the water to drip out.

Drip watering systems allow pinpoint application of water. Water is applied at a rate the soil can absorb, eliminating runoff. The soil between your new plants stays dry, discouraging weeds.

Fertilizing

Most vines need very little fertilizer. If leaves, especially older ones, become yellow, the vine needs nitrogen. Any good general purpose plant food such as a 10-10-10 (10% nitrogen, 10% phosphorus, and 10% potassium) will correct the deficiency.

The specific fertilizer product you use will include directions, but as a general guide, 4 tablespoons of a 10-10-10 fertilizer per established vine is plenty.

Mulching

Mulching is one of the best things you can do for your vines and your garden in general. A mulch is a layer of material placed on top of soil to cover and protect it, and conserve moisture. A mulch keeps soil cool and prevents it from baking and cracking. Delicate feeder roots that cannot tolerate hot soil are then free to explore the more nutritious soil surface.

Mulching also helps prevent weeds by covering their seeds. Weeds that do manage to penetrate a mulch layer are easy to pull because the soil around them is loose.

The most common mulches are fir bark, sawdust, pine needles, and compost. But any organic material that does not compress and exclude air is a possible mulch. Apply a mulch about 2 inches deep right after planting. You will need seven to eight 2-cubic-foot bags to cover 100 square feet to a 2-inch depth.

Pruning

Prune vines to keep them in bounds and to promote or enhance flowering. Most vines require some regular pruning. Special pruning needs of different vines are noted in specific plant listings in the encyclopedia.

Basics: Always remove any dead or broken branches. These are unattractive, block light from new growth, and invite pest infestation. Every vine, regardless of how much or how little other pruning it requires, should be cleaned up this way each spring.

Pruning for flowers: There are basically two kinds of flowering vines and the differences between them determine when each is pruned. Some flowering vines, such as wisteria, flower on old growth. Prune these vines during the dormant season. Prune vines that flower on last season's growth, such as evergreen clematis, after flowering. Pruning at that time gives them a full season to make new growth and new flower buds. If pruned in the winter or spring before flowering, flower buds are removed.

Other vines, such as silver lace vine, make flowers on their current season's growth. These vines typically flower in late spring, summer, or fall. Prune such vines in fall or early spring before new growth starts.

Prune woody, non-flowering vines such as English ivy or Boston ivy once a year in early spring.

Pruning for renewal: Severe renewal pruning is the only recourse if a vine is seriously overgrown. Cut it off at ground level in early spring and new growth will quickly fill back in. Use a pruning saw if necessary to remove all stems to within a few inches of the soil. Similar but less drastic treatment of plants that climb with long arching canes, such as climbing roses, will improve their flower show. Cut out the oldest, dark-colored canes to ground level. Renewal is best done in early spring just before new growth begins. This stimulates vigorous growth and more abundant flower production.

Problems and Solutions

Some vines are subject to attack by fungus or bacterial diseases, or by insect pests such as aphids, caterpillars, mealybugs, scale, and spider mites. Any severe pest problems a vine might have are mentioned in the encyclopedia section. There is also a column in the care chart on page 62 that indicates whether or not a vine is generally considered pest-resistant. If you use this information as a guide when selecting plants, you can help eliminate many potential problems.

Insect pests and diseases can be controlled chemically, physically, or biologically. The trend in recent years has been away from chemical spraying in favor of physical controls—such as hosing pests off—and biological controls—encouraging useful insects such as ladybugs and lacewings to stay in your garden. It is not possible in a book of this size to recommend specific treatment programs for every garden pest. Also, the effectiveness of control measures will vary, depending on the season, region, and the type of weather when treatment is administered.

Good garden maintenance practices, and close, regular observation of the plants in your garden can help minimize problems. Early detection of insect and disease pests and prompt treatment can help keep problems from becoming serious.

If you spot symptoms of pest infestations, such as the cottony masses of mealybugs, dying flower shoots and branches, spotted leaves, or other unusual changes in vine growth, cut off a small portion of the infected plant and take the cutting to your garden center. Your nurseryman can usually identify the problem and recommend an effective treatment program.

Another good source of information on plant pests is your County Agricultural or Extension Agent. To locate that office, look in your phone book under the name of your county for the Cooperative Extension Service listing.

Pruning

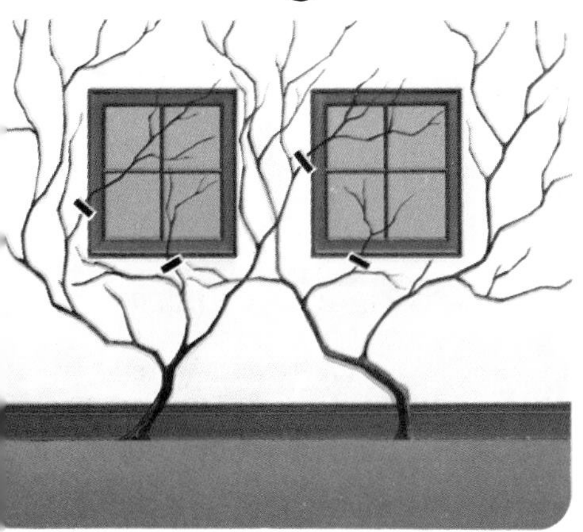

Control growth of woody vines, such as English ivy, by cutting back wayward branches as needed.

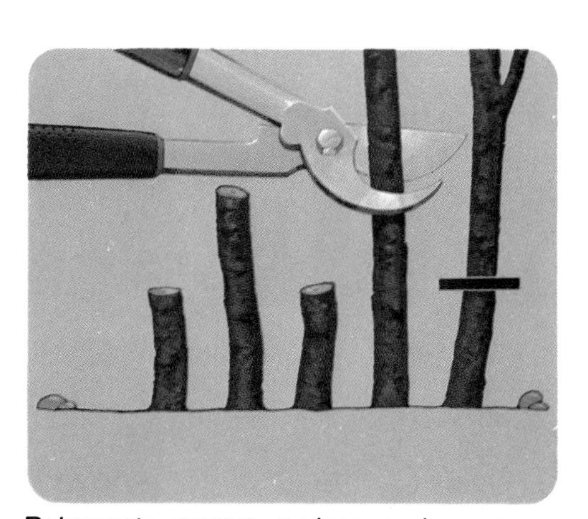

Rejuvenate overgrown vines, such as roses, by cutting back all stems to ground level in early spring.

To promote branching and dense growth of vines such as clematis, pinch back tips after flowering.

Prune wisteria in winter when the plant is dormant by removing seed pods and thinning tangled branches.

At the same time, shorten the flowering branches of wisteria, leaving short "spurs", as shown above.

After pruning, the shortened spurs, branches, and main stems of wisteria should look like the illustration above.

Problems and Solutions

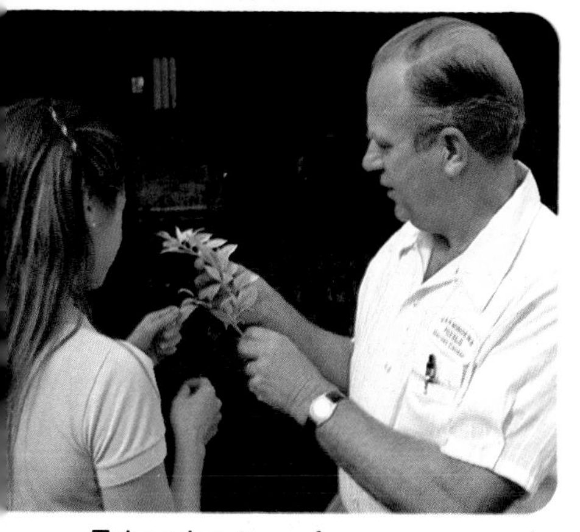

Take advantage of your nurseryman's gardening expertise.

Chlorosis retards plant growth. It is characterized by yellowing of foliage between leaf veins.

A chlorotic condition can be corrected by spraying foliage with a fertilizer containing chelated iron.

Planting and Care of Vines

This chart presents in simplified form basic information about the planting requirements and follow-up care for each of the vines discussed in this book. Use it as a quick reference to determine what conditions and care the vines you select will need to grow successfully. More detailed information on planting and care of particular plants is contained in the encyclopedia section.

	Exposure			Water			Soil					Fertilizer			Pruning			Pest Resistant
PLANT NAME	Sun	Partial Shade	Shade	Plenty	Regular	Drought Tolerant	Acid	Alkaline	Well-drained	Fertile	Infertile	Heavy	Regular	Light	Heading	Thinning	Season	
Actinidia chinensis	■	■		■	■		■	■	■	■		■	■		■		dormant	no
Antigonon leptopus	■				■	■		■			■			■	■[5]	■	dormant	yes
Beaumontia grandiflora	■			■	■		■	■	■	■		■				■	fall[6]	yes
Bougainvillea sp.	■				■	■	■	■	■	■	■			■		■	summer[6]	no
Campsis sp.	■				■	■	■	■	■		■			■	■	■	dormant	yes
Celastrus sp.	■	■			■	■	■	■	■	■	■		■	■		■	spring[8]	no
Clematis armandii	■	■			■			■[3]	■	■			■		■[5]	■	spring[6]	no
Clematis x jackmanii	■	■		■	■			■	■	■			■		■[5]	■	spring[8]	no
Clematis texensis	■	■			■	■		■	■	■			■		■[5]	■	spring[8]	no
Clytostoma callistegioides	■	■	■		■		■	■	■	■			■			■	dormant[7]	yes
Distictis sp.	■	■[1]			■		■	■	■	■			■			■	summer[6]	yes
Euonymus fortunei	■	■		■	■	■	■	■	■	■	■		■	■	■[4]	■	spring	no
x Fatshedera lizei	■	■	■	■	■		■	■	■	■			■		■[2]	■	anytime	no
Ficus pumila	■	■			■	■	■	■	■	■			■			■	anytime	yes
Gelsemium sempervirens	■	■			■	■	■	■	■	■			■	■		■	fall	yes
Hedera sp.	■	■	■	■	■	■	■[3]	■	■	■	■			■	■	■[4]	spring[8]	no
Hibbertia scandens	■	■		■	■		■	■	■	■			■			■	spring or fall	yes
Hydrangea anomala	■	■		■	■	■	■		■	■			■			■	dormant[7]	yes
Jasminum sp.	■	■		■	■		■	■	■	■			■			■	summer[6]	yes
Lonicera hildebrandiana	■	■		■	■		■	■	■	■	■		■	■	■	■	summer[6]	yes
Lonicera japonica	■	■	■		■	■	■	■		■	■			■	■	■	spring[8] or fall	yes
Lonicera sempervirens	■	■			■	■	■	■	■	■	■			■	■	■	summer[6]	no
Parthenocissus sp.	■	■	■	■	■	■	■	■	■	■	■		■	■	■[5]	■	spring[8]	no
Passiflora sp.	■				■		■	■	■	■			■		■[5]	■	fall	no
Polygonum aubertii	■	■			■	■	■	■	■		■			■	■[5]	■	fall[8]	yes
Rhoicissus capensis		■	■		■		■	■	■	■			■	■	■[2]	■	spring[8] or fall	no
Rosa hybrids	■	■		■	■		■		■	■		■	■		■	■	dormant[7]	no
Tecomaria capensis	■	■			■	■		■	■	■	■		■	■		■	dormant[7]	yes
Trachelospermum sp.	■	■		■	■		■	■	■	■			■		■	■[4]	summer[6]	no
Vitis sp.	■			■	■	■	■[3]	■	■		■		■	■	■	■	dormant	no
Wisteria sp.	■				■		■	■	■	■	■		■	■		■	dormant[7]	yes

[1] — Partial shade inland; [2] — Pinch tips; [3] — Neutral to alkaline soil preferred; [4] — Takes shearing; [5] — Cut old stems to base to renew; [6] — After flowering; [7] — Late winter; [8] — Early spring

Name Cross-Reference

A plant can have many common names but has only *one* proper botanical or scientific name. Some botanical names, because of their Latin origin, may be difficult to pronounce and remember at first, but become easier to use and more interesting as you become familiar with them. Common English plant names are often helpfully descriptive but they are too variable from person-to-person and place-to-place to be relied upon. The following list matches the most often used common names of flowering trees to their proper botanical names.

The parts of a botanical name that gardeners need to understand are the *genus*, *species*, and *cultivar* (or variety). The genus name signifies the general group to which the plant belongs, and together with the species name describes a particular plant. For instance, all figs belong to the genus *Ficus*, and *Ficus pumila* is the botanical name for the creeping fig.

The cultivar is the capitalized name between single quotation marks, for instance 'Gold Heart' in *Hedera helix* 'Gold Heart'. Cultivar stands for a cultivated variety. A cultivar is a plant that is propagated because of an outstanding feature that may or may not be perpetuated in nature. The cultivar may differ only slightly from the species or it may have significant differences, such as plant form, leaf color, or flower color. Botanical names that have an x between the genus and species, such as *Passiflora x alatocaerulea*, indicate the plant is a hybrid between two species, formed either naturally or by breeders.

Common Name	Botanical Name
Algerian Ivy	*Hedera canariensis*
Bittersweet, American	*Celastrus scandens*
Bittersweet, Evergreen	*Euonymus fortunei*
Bittersweet, Oriental	*Celastrus orbiculatus*
Boston Ivy	*Parthenocissus tricuspidata*
Botanical-Wonder	*x Fatshedera lizei*
Bougainvillea	*Bougainvillea sp.*
Cape Grape	*Rhoicissus capensis*
Cape Honeysuckle	*Tecomaria capensis*
Chinese Gooseberry	*Actinidia chinensis*
Chinese Trumpet Creeper	*Campsis grandiflora*
Clematis, Armand	*Clematis armandii*
Clematis, Evergreen	*Clematis armandii*
Clematis, Jackman	*Clematis x jackmanii*
Clematis, Scarlet	*Clematis texensis*
Corallita	*Antigonon leptopus*
Coral Vine	*Antigonon leptopus*
Easter-Lily Vine	*Beaumontia grandiflora*
Euonymus, Purple-Leaf	*Euonymus fortunei* 'Colorata'
European Grape	*Vitis vinifera*
Evergreen Bittersweet	*Euonymus fortunei*
Evergreen Grape	*Rhoicissus capensis*
Fatshedera	*x Fatshedera lizei*
Fig, Creeping	*Ficus pumila*
Fleece Flower	*Polygonum aubertii*
Fox Grape	*Vitis labrusca*
Gold Guinea Plant	*Hibbertia scandens*
Grape, American	*Vitis labrusca*
Grape, Cape	*Rhoicissus capensis*
Grape, European	*Vitis vinifera*
Grape, Evergreen	*Rhoicissus capensis*
Grape, Fox	*Vitis labrusca*
Grape, Muscadine	*Vitis rotundifolia*
Herald's-Trumpet	*Beaumontia grandiflora*
Honeysuckle, Cape	*Tecomaria capensis*
Honeysuckle, Giant Burmese	*Lonicera hildebrandiana*
Honeysuckle, Hall's Japanese	*Lonicera japonica* 'Halliana'
Honeysuckle, Japanese	*Lonicera japonica*
Honeysuckle, Trumpet	*Lonicera sempervirens*
Hydrangea, Climbing	*Hydrangea anomala*
Ivy, Algerian	*Hedera canariensis*
Ivy, Boston	*Parthenocissus tricuspidata*
Ivy, English	*Hedera helix*
Jasmine, Angel-Wing	*Jasminum nitidum*
Jasmine, Chinese	*Jasminum polyanthum*
Jasmine, Confederate	*Trachelospermum jasminoides*
Jasmine, Star	*Trachelospermum jasminoides*
Jasmine, Yellow Star	*Trachelospermum asiaticum*
Jessamine, Carolina Yellow	*Gelsemium sempervirens*
Kiwi	*Actinidia chinensis*
Madame Galen Trumpet Creeper	*Campsis x tagliabuana* 'Madame Galen'
Muscadine Grape	*Vitis rotundifolia*
Oriental Bittersweet	*Celastrus orbiculatus*
Passionflower, Blue	*Passiflora caerulea*
Passionflower, Hybrid	*Passiflora x alatocaerulea*
Passion Fruit	*Passiflora edulis*
Purple Granadilla	*Passiflora edulis*
Queen's-Wreath	*Antigonon leptopus*
Rose, Climbing	*Rosa* hybrids
Rosa de Montaña	*Antigonon leptopus*
Rose, Mountain	*Antigonon leptopus*
Scuppernong	*Vitis rotundifolia*
Silver Lace Vine	*Polygonum aubertii*
Trumpet Creeper, Chinese	*Campsis grandiflora*
Trumpet Creeper, Madame Galen	*Campsis x tagliabuana* 'Madame Galen'
Trumpet Creeper Vine	*Campsis radicans*
Trumpet Vine, Blood-Red	*Distictis buccinatoria*
Trumpet Vine, Vanilla	*Distictis laxiflora*
Trumpet Vine, Violet	*Clytostoma callistegioides*
Virginia Creeper	*Parthenocissus quinquefolia*
Wintercreeper	*Euonymus fortunei*
Wisteria, Chinese	*Wisteria sinensis*
Wisteria, Japanese	*Wisteria floribunda*
Yang-Tao	*Actinidia chinensis*

Index

Main plant listings indicated by bold numbers.

B C D E F